Imperial County, California

Johnathan Black

Contents

Articles

Transportation 153

References

Overview of the County

Imperial County, California

County of Imperial
— County —
The fields of Imperial Valley
Seal
Location in the state of California
California's location in the United States |

Country	United States
State	California
Region	Imperial Valley

Incorporated	1907
County seat	El Centro
Largest city	El Centro
Area	
- Total	4482 sq mi (11608.3 km^2)
- Land	4175 sq mi (10813.2 km^2)
- Water	307 sq mi (795.1 km^2)
Population (2008 Est.)	163972
- Density	34/sq mi (13.1/km^2)
Time zone	Pacific Standard Time (UTC-8)
- Summer (DST)	Pacific Daylight Time (UTC-7)
Website	www.imperialcounty.net [1]

Imperial County is a county located in the Imperial Valley, in the far southeast of the U.S. state of California, bordering both Arizona and Mexico. It is part of the El Centro, California Metropolitan Statistical Area which encompasses all of Imperial County. The population as of 2000 was 142,361. The county seat is the city of El Centro. Established in 1907, it was the last county to be established in California. Imperial County is also part of the Southern California border region, also referred to as San Diego-Imperial, the smallest but most economically diverse region in the state.

Although this region is a desert, with high temperatures and low average rainfall of three inches (seventy-five mm) per year, the economy is heavily based on agriculture due to irrigation, supplied wholly from the Colorado River via the All-American Canal.

The Imperial Valley is a melting pot of White American and Hispanic cultures. On the U.S. side, the majority of residents are of Mexican American or Latino heritage, while the Mexican side was greatly influenced by American culture for many decades. The entire valley has multi-racial representation of African Americans, European Americans, East Asian Americans, South Asian Americans, and Native Americans.

History

Juan Bautista de Anza
Bezerra Nieto

Spanish explorer Melchior Díaz was one of the first Europeans to visit the area around Imperial Valley in 1540. The explorer Juan Bautista de Anza also explored the area in 1776. Years later, after the Mexican-American War, the northern half of the valley was annexed by the U.S., while the southern half remained under Mexican rule. Small scale settlement in natural aquifer areas occurred in the early 1800s (the present-day site of Mexicali), but most permanent settlement (Anglo Americans in the U.S. side, Mexicans in the other side) was after 1900.

In 1905, torrential rainfall in the American Southwest caused the Colorado River (the only drainage for the region) to flood, including canals that had been built to irrigate the Imperial Valley. Since the valley is partially below sea level, the waters never fully receded, but collected in the Salton Sink in what is now called the Salton Sea, the world's only artificial inland sea.

Imperial County was formed in 1907 from the eastern portion of San Diego County. The county took its name from Imperial Valley, itself named for the Imperial Land Company, a subsidiary of the California Development Company, which at the turn of the 20th century had claimed the southern portion of the Colorado desert for agriculture. Much of the Imperial Land Company's land also existed in Mexico (Baja California). The objective of the company was commercial crop farming development.

By 1910, the land company had managed to settle and develop thousands of farms on both sides of the border. But the Mexican Revolution severely disrupted the company's plans. Nearly 10,000 farmers and their families in Mexico were ethnically cleansed by the rival Mexican armies. Not until the 1920s was the other side of California in America sufficiently peaceful and prosperous for the company to earn a return for a large percentage of Mexicans, but some chose to stay and lay down roots in newly sprouted communities in the valley.

The county experienced a period of migration of "Okies" from drought-trodden dust bowl farms by the need of migrant labor, and prosperous job-seekers alike from across the U.S. arrived in the 1930s and 1940s, especially in World War II and after the completion of the All American Canal from its source, the Colorado River, from 1948 to 1951. By the 1950 census, over 50,000 residents lived in Imperial County alone, about 40 times that of 1910. Most of the population was year-round but would increase every winter by migrant laborers from Mexico. Until the 1960s, the farms in Imperial County provided substantial economic returns to the company and the valley.

Sites of interest

Fort Yuma

Fort Yuma is located on the banks of the Colorado River in Winterhaven, California. First established after the end of the Mexican-American War in 1848, it was originally located in the bottoms near the Colorado River, less than 1 mile (2 km) below the mouth of the Gila River. It was to defend the newly settled community of Yuma, Arizona on the other side of the Colorado River and the nearby Mexican border. In March 1851 the post was moved to a small elevation on the Colorado's west bank, opposite the present city of Yuma, Arizona, on the site of the former Mission Puerto de Purísima Concepción. This site had been occupied by Camp Calhoun, named for John C. Calhoun, established in 1849. Fort Yuma was established to protect the southern emigrant travel route to California and to attempt control of the warlike Yuma Indians in the surrounding 100-mile (160 km) area.

Blue Angels

NAF El Centro is the winter home of the U.S. Navy Flight Demonstration Squadron, The Blue Angels. NAF El Centro historically kicks off the Blue Angels' season with their first air show, traditionally held in March.

Imperial Valley Expo & fairgrounds

Home to the California Mid-Winter Fair and Fiesta which is the local county fair. It is also home to the Imperial Valley Speedway, a race track of $3/8$ miles (600 m).

Blue Angels

Algodones Sand Dunes

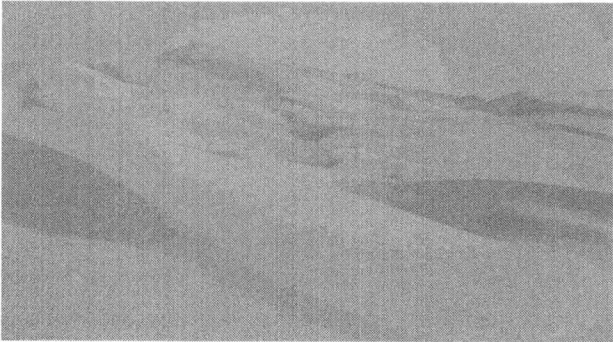
The Algodones Dunes

The name Algodones Dunes refers to the entire geographic feature, while the administrative designation for that portion managed by the Bureau of Land Management is the "Imperial Sand Dunes Recreation Area" (sometimes called the "Glamis Dunes"). The Algodones Sand Dunes are the largest mass of sand dunes in California. This dune system extends for more than 40 miles (60 km) along the eastern edge of the Imperial Valley agricultural region in a band averaging 5 miles (8 km) in width. A major east-west route of the Union Pacific railroad skirts the eastern edge.The dune system is divided into 3 areas. The northern most area is known as Mammoth Wash. South of Mammoth Wash is the North Algodones Dunes Wilderness established by the 1994 California Desert Protection Act. This area is closed to motorized use and access is by hiking and horseback. The largest and most heavily used area begins at Highway 78 and continues south just past Interstate 8. The expansive dune formations offer picturesque scenery,, a chance to view rare plants and animals, and a playground for ATV and off-roading enthusiasts. The dunes are also popular in film making and have been the site for movies such as Return of the Jedi.

Colorado River

The Colorado River is a river in the southwestern United States and northwestern Mexico, approximately 2,330 kilometres (1,450 mi) long, draining a part of the arid regions on the western slope of the Rocky Mountains. The natural course of the river flows from north of Grand Lake, Colorado into the Gulf of California. For many months out of the year, however, no water actually flows from the United States to the gulf, due to human consumption. The river is a popular destination for water sports including fishing, boating, water-skiing, and jet-skiing.

Salvation Mountain

Salvation Mountain (location 33°15′14.9″N 115°28′21.4″W) is a colorful artificial mountain north of Calipatria, California, near Slab City. It is made from adobe, straw, and thousands of gallons of paint. It was created by Leonard Knight to convey the message that "God Loves Everyone". Knight refused substantial donations of money and labor from supporters who wished to modify his message of universal love to favor or disfavor particular groups.

Anza-Borrego Desert State Park

Bighorn Sheep at Palm Canyon in Anza-Borrego State Park

Anza-Borrego Desert State Park, portions of which are located in Imperial County, is the largest state park in California. 500 miles (800 km) of dirt roads, 12 wilderness areas and miles of hiking trails provide visitors with an unparalleled opportunity to experience the wonders of the Colorado Desert. The park is named after Spanish explorer Juan Bautista de Anza and the Spanish name borrego, or bighorn sheep. The park features washes, wildflowers, palm groves, cacti and sweeping vistas. Visitors may also have the chance to see roadrunner, golden eagles, kit foxes, mule deer and bighorn sheep as well as iguanas, chuckwallas and the red diamond rattlesnake.

Fossil Canyon and Painted Gorge

Located near Ocotillo, California in the Coyote Mountains, Fossil Canyon and the surrounding area is a great place for rock hounding and fossil hunting. The fossils here are not dinosaurs, but ancient shells, coral, and oysters from the Miocene epoch when the area was underwater.

The Painted Gorge, located on the eastern side of the Coyote Mountains, consists of sedimentary, metamorphic and igneous rocks. Heat and movement over time has created fantastic shapes and colors. Oranges, reds, purples, and mauves mixed with browns and blacks create a palette of color as the sun illuminates and plays shadows upon this geologic wonder.

Imperial NWR

The Imperial National Wildlife Refuge protects wildlife habitat along 30 miles (50 km) of the lower Colorado River in Arizona and California, including the last un-channeled section before the river enters Mexico. The river and its associated backwater lakes and wetlands are a green oasis, contrasting with the surrounding desert mountains. It is a refuge and breeding area for migratory birds and local desert wildlife.

Sonny Bono Salton Sea NWR

The Sonny Bono Salton Sea National Wildlife Refuge is located 40 miles (60 km) north of the Mexican border at the southern end of the Salton Sea in California's Imperial Valley. Situated along the Pacific Flyway, the refuge is the only one of its kind, located 227 feet below sea level. Because of its southern latitude, elevation and location in the Colorado Desert, the refuge experiences some of the highest temperatures in the nation. Daily temperatures from May to October generally exceed 100°F with temperatures of 116°-120°F recorded yearly.

Mexicali

Mexico (the border city of Mexicali, Baja California) offers big city amenities like museums, a zoo, a sports convention center, and an international airport. Visitors cross by foot or car from Calexico in the United States every day. Restaurants and taco stands, pharmacies, bars and dance clubs are part of the draw for the city's tourists. Many shops and stalls selling Mexican crafts and souvenirs are also located in walking distance from the border. Also many residents from California, Arizona and Nevada look for medical and dental services in Mexicali, because they tend to be less expensive than those in the United States. Mexico's drinking age of 18 (vs. 21 in the United States) makes it a common weekend destination for many high school and college aged Southern Californians.

Geography

According to the U.S. Census Bureau, the county has a total area of 4,482 square miles (11,608 km²), of which 4,175 square miles (10,812 km²) is land and 307 square miles (795 km²) (6.85%) is water. Much of Imperial County is below sea level.

The county is in the Colorado Desert, an extension of the larger Sonoran Desert.

The Colorado River forms the county's eastern boundary. Two notable geographic features are found in the county, the Salton Sea, at 235 feet (72 m) below sea level, and the Algodones Dunes, one of the largest dune fields in America.

The Chocolate Mountains are located east of the Salton Sea, and extend in a northwest-southeast direction for approximately 60 miles (97 km).

In this region, the geology is dominated by the transition of the tectonic plate boundary from rift to fault. The southernmost strands of the San Andreas Fault connect the northern-most extensions of the East Pacific Rise. Consequently, the region is subject to earthquakes, and the crust is being stretched, resulting in a sinking of the terrain over time.

Cities

Towns over 5,000 population

- **El Centro** - 40,563
- Calexico - 27,109
- Brawley - 22,052
- Imperial - 11,754
- Calipatria - 7,289
- Holtville - 5,612

Towns over 1,000 population

- Heber - 2,566
- Westmorland - 2,131
- Seeley - 1,624
- Niland - 1,143
- Salton City - 1,143

Towns under 1,000 population

- Desert Shores - 792
- Winterhaven - 529
- Salton Sea Beach - 392
- Bombay Beach - 366
- Ocotillo - 296
- Palo Verde - 236

National protected areas

- Cibola National Wildlife Refuge (part)
- Imperial National Wildlife Refuge (part)
- Sonny Bono Salton Sea National Wildlife Refuge

Codes for Imperial

Area Codes

Main article: List of California area codes

760 - Covers all of the El Centro metropolitan area as well as Palm Springs, Oceanside, Bishop, Ridgecrest, Barstow, Needles; northern San Diego County, and southeastern California, including much of the Mojave Desert and the Owens Valley. (Split from 619 on March 22, 1997, overlayed by area code 442 in 2009)

Zip Codes

- 92243 in El Centro, CA • 43,744

- 92231 in Calexico, CA • 27,792

- 92227 in Brawley, CA • 23,419

- 92251 in Imperial, CA • 14,469

- 92250 in Holtville, CA • 8,038

- 92233 in Calipatria, CA • 7,854

- 92283 in Winterhaven, CA • 3,622

- 92249 in Heber, CA • 3,558

- 92257 in Bombay Beach, CA • 2,710

- 92281 in Westmorland, CA • 2,362

- 92273 in Seeley, CA • 1,588

- 92275 in Salton City, CA • 803

- 92259 in Ocotillo, CA • 500

- 92266 in Palo Verde, CA • 340

Economy

Thousands of acres of prime farmland have transformed the desert into one of the most productive farming regions in California with an annual crop production of over $1 billion. Agriculture is the largest industry in Imperial County and accounts for 48% of all employment. Although this region is a desert, with high temperatures and low average rainfall of three inches (seventy-five mm) per year, the economy is heavily based on agriculture due to irrigation, which is supplied wholly from the Colorado River via the All-American Canal. A vast system of canals, check dams, and pipelines carry the water all over the valley, a system which forms the Imperial Irrigation District, or IID. The water distribution system includes over 1,400 miles (2,300 km) of canal and with 1,100 miles (1,800 km) of pipeline. The number of canal and pipeline branches number roughly over a hundred. Imported water and a long growing season allow two crop cycles each year, and the Imperial Valley is a major source of winter fruits and vegetables, cotton, and grain for U.S. and international markets. Alfalfa is another major crop produced in the Imperial Valley. The agricultural lands are served by a constructed agricultural drain system, which conveys surface runoff and subsurface drainage from fields to the Salton Sea, which is a designated repository for agricultural runoff.

El Centro is the commercial center of Imperial County. Fifty percent of the jobs in El Centro come from the service and retail sector.

A recent growth in the interest of Imperial County as a filming location, has spurred growth in servicing this industry. Due to its desert environment and proximity to Los Angeles, California, movies are sometimes filmed in the sand dunes outside the agricultural portions of the Imperial County. These have included *Return of the Jedi*, *Stargate*, *The Scorpion King*, and *Into the Wild*. Additionally, portions of the 2005 film *Jarhead* were filmed here because of its similarity to the desert terrain of Iraq.

Renewable energy source

Imperial Valley has become a hotbed of renewable energy projects, both solar and geothermal. This is driven in part by California's mandate to generate 20% of its power from renewable sources by the end of 2010, the valley's excellent sun resources, the high unemployment, its proximity to large population centers on the coast, and large tracts of otherwise unusable desert land. Much of the land suitable for green energy is owned by the federal government (Bureau of Land Management). As of April 2008, the BLM has received 163 applications to build renewable energy projects on 1600000 acres (6500 km^2) in California, "almost all of them are planned for the Imperial Valley and the desert region north of the valley." Stirling Energy is currently building one of the world's largest solar thermal plants, 10 square miles (26 km^2) with 38,000 "sun catchers," it will power up to 600,000 homes once it is fully operational by around 2015. CalEnergy currently runs a geothermal plant that generates enough power for 300,000 homes and could tap into more for up to 2.5 million homes.

Transportation infrastructure

Major highways

- Interstate 8
- State Route 7
- State Route 78
- State Route 86
- State Route 98
- State Route 111
- State Route 115

Public transportation

Imperial County is served by Greyhound Lines and Imperial Valley Transit buses. Amtrak trains also travel through the county, but with no scheduled stops.

Airports

- Imperial County Airport, located just north of El Centro, is the main airport in the county. It is primarily a general aviation airport with limited commercial flight service.
- Holtville Airport is a general aviation airport located roughly 5 miles (8 km) east of Holtville.
- Calexico Airport is located 15 miles (24 km) south of Interstate 8 on State Route 111. It is a general aviation field, used in part to service maquiladora factories in nearby Mexicali.

Demographics

The Imperial County is a blend of White American and Hispanic cultures. On the U.S. side, the majority of residents are of Mexican American or Latino heritage, while the Mexican side has been greatly influenced by the culture of the United States for many decades. The valley's population contains communities of African, European, East and South Asian, and Native American ancestry.

As of the census of 2000, there were 142,361 people, 39,384 households, and 31,467 families residing in the county. The population density was 34 people per square mile (13/km²). There were 43,891 housing units at an average density of 10 per square mile (4/km²). The racial makeup of the county was 49.37% White, 3.95% Black or African American, 1.87% Native American, 1.99% Asian, 0.08% Pacific Islander, 39.08% from other races, and 3.65% from two or more races. 72.22% of the population were Hispanic or Latino of any race. 65.7% spoke Spanish as their first language and 32.3% English.

By 2005 the estimated percentage of non-Hispanic whites in the county was 18%. The percentage of Hispanics had risen to 75.3. The African American percentage now stood at 4.2%, showing that this population was growing significantly in the county. The number of Hispanics had increased by 10 times since the census of 1910. There are third- and fourth-generation Mexican Americans in the county who identify more with general American culture but have preserved their Hispanic heritage, such as usage of the Spanish language.

Imperial County has a long-established Asian American community, although small in number compared with urban centers in California. Mainly of Chinese, but also of Filipino, Japanese, Korean and a scant number of Southeast Asian ancestry, often are descendants of railroad workers, ditch diggers and farm laborers in the early 20th century, some arrived through the Mexican border. Imperial County is also home to 10,000 Indian Americans, the highest number outside a major U.S. city, and they provided some Indian features in a mainly Latin American culture.

There were 39,384 households out of which 46.7% had children under the age of 18 living with them, 57.7% were married couples living together, 17.1% had a female householder with no husband present, and 20.1% were non-families. 17.1% of all households were made up of individuals and 8.1% had someone living alone who was 65 years of age or older. The average household size was 3.33 and the average family size was 3.77.

In the county the population was spread out with 31.4% under the age of 18, 9.9% from 18 to 24, 30.4% from 25 to 44, 18.2% from 45 to 64, and 10.0% who were 65 years of age or older. The median age was 31 years. For every 100 females there were 109.3 males. For every 100 females age 18 and over, there were 111.4 males.

The median income for a household in the county was $31,870, and the median income for a family was $35,226. Males had a median income of $32,775 versus $23,974 for females. The per capita income for the county was $13,239. About 19.4% of families and 22.6% of the population were below the poverty line, including 28.7% of those under age 18 and 13.6% of those age 65 or over.

According to Wikipedia, Imperial County has the lowest per capita income of any county in California.

By 2006 the population had risen to 160,201, the population growth rate since the year 2000 was 30%, the highest in California and fifth highest in the United States in the time period. High levels of immigration, new residents search for affordable homes, and a search for retirement homes can explain the population increase.

Politics

Presidential election results

Year	DEM	GOP	Others
2008	**62.2%** *24,162*	36.1% *14,008*	1.7% *650*
2004	**52.4%** *17,964*	46.4% *15,890*	1.2% *420*
2000	**53.5%** *15,489*	43.3% *12,524*	3.2% *924*
1996	**55.3%** *14,591*	36.8% *9,705*	8.0% *2,104*
1992	**43.9%** *11,109*	38.5% *9,759*	17.6% *4,450*
1988	43.8% *10,243*	**55.2%** *12,889*	1.0% *233*
1984	36.9% *8,237*	**62.0%** *13,829*	1.1% *235*
1980	36.9% *7,961*	**55.9%** *12,068*	7.2% *1,550*
1976	48.2% *10,244*	**49.9%** *10,618*	1.9% *400*
1972	34.9% *7,982*	**62.1%** *14,178*	3.0% *689*
1968	36.6% *7,481*	**52.9%** *10,818*	10.5% *2,147*

| 1964 | **51.8%** *11,143* | 48.1% *10,330* | 0.1% *19* |
| 1960 | 46.0% *9,119* | **53.6%** *10,606* | 0.4% *81* |

Imperial County is a Democratic stronghold in presidential, congressional and local elections. The last Republican to win a majority in the county was George H. W. Bush in 1988.

On November 4, 2008, Imperial County voted 69.7% for Proposition 8, which amended the California Constitution to ban same-sex marriages, showing more support for the proposition than any other strongly Democratic county. After being declared unconstitutional by a lower federal court, Imperial County continues to defend Proposition 8 in the federal judicial system.

Imperial is part of California's 51st congressional district, which is held by Democrat Bob Filner. In the state legislature, Imperial is part of the 80th Assembly district, which is held by Democrat Manuel Perez, and the 40th Senate district, which is held by Democrat Denise Ducheny.

In popular culture

- Dimmsdale is a fictional city located in Imperial County that is shown on the Nickelodeon animated series *The Fairly OddParents*.
- Scenes for the 2006 film *Borat: Cultural Learnings of America for Make Benefit Glorious Nation of Kazakhstan* were filmed in Imperial County, but were not used in the finished film.
- The majority of *Jarhead* and *the Salton Sea* was filmed in the Imperial Valley.
- Scenes from *Star Wars* were filmed in the Imperial Valley sand dunes, *Top Gun* were also filmed in the El Centro Naval Air Station and *Independence Day* was located in the Imperial Valley.
- Rock en Espanol group Calexico glean their name from the Imperial Valley border town that ajoins Mexicali, Baja California of Mexico.
- Imperial, by William T. Vollmann, published July 30, 2009, documents the history and culture of Imperial County, California. A companion volume of photographs was published August 18, 2009.

See also

- El Centro Metropolitan Area
- Category: Geography of Imperial County, California

External links

- Official Imperial County website [2]
- Website for the City of Imperial, California [3]
- Imperial Irrigation District [4]
- Imperial Valley Economic Development Corporation [5]
- Imperial Valley Living [6]

- Statistical profile of Imperial County, California [7]

Geographical coordinates: 33°02′N 115°21′W

California

State of California	
Flag	Seal
Nickname(s): *The Golden State*	
Motto(s): *Eureka*	
Official language(s)	English
Demonym	Californian
Capital	Sacramento
Largest city	Los Angeles
Largest metro area	Greater Los Angeles
Area	Ranked 3rd in the US

- Total	163,696 sq mi (423,970 km^2)
- Width	250 miles (400 km)
- Length	770 miles (1,240 km)
- % water	4.7
- Latitude	32° 32′ N to 42° N
- Longitude	114° 8′ W to 124° 26′ W
Population	Ranked 1st in the US
- Total	36,961,664 (2009 est.) 33,871,648 (2000)
- Density	234.4/sq mi (90.49/km^2) Ranked 11th in the US
- Median income	US$61,021 (9th)
Elevation	
- Highest point	Mount Whitney 14,494 ft (4,418 m)
- Mean	2,900 ft (884 m)
- Lowest point	Death Valley -282 ft (-86 m)
Admission to Union	September 9, 1850 (31st)
Governor	Arnold Schwarzenegger (R)
Lieutenant Governor	Abel Maldonado (R)
Legislature	State Legislature
- Upper house	State Senate
- Lower house	State Assembly
U.S. Senators	Dianne Feinstein (D) Barbara Boxer (D)
U.S. House delegation	34 Democrats, 19 Republicans (list)
Time zone	Pacific: UTC-8/-7
Abbreviations	CA Calif. US-CA
Website	http://ca.gov/

California State Symbols

The Flag of California.

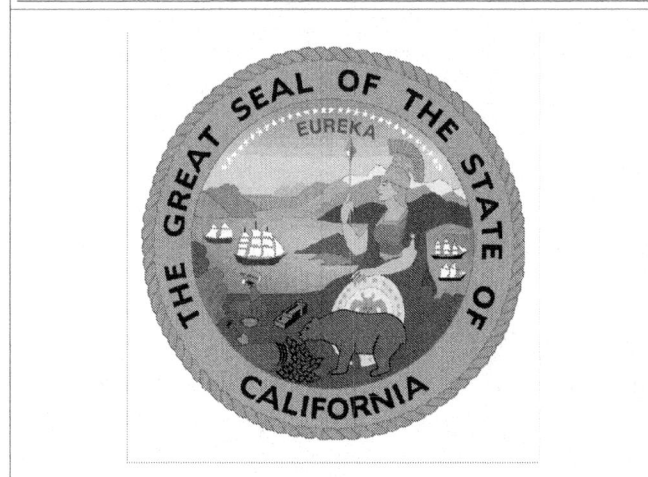

The Seal of California.

Animate insignia

Bird(s)	California Quail
Fish	Golden Trout
Flower(s)	California Poppy
Grass	Purple Needlegrass
Insect	California Dogface Butterfly
Mammal(s)	California grizzly bear (State Animal)

Reptile	Desert Tortoise
Tree	California Redwood

Inanimate insignia	
Beverage	Wine
Colors	Blue & Gold
Dance	West Coast Swing
Fossil	Sabre-toothed cat
Gemstone	Benitoite
Mineral	Native Gold
Rock	Serpentine
Soil	San Joaquin
Song(s)	"I Love You, California"
Tartan	California State Tartan

Route marker(s)

State Quarter
Released in 2005

Lists of United States state insignia

California (pronounced [i] /kælɪˈfɔrnjə/) is the most populous state in the United States and the third-largest by land area, after Alaska and Texas. California is also the most populous sub-national entity in North America. It's on the U.S. West Coast, bordered by the Pacific Ocean to the west and by the states of Oregon to the north, Nevada to the east, Arizona to the southeast, Baja California, Mexico, to the south. Its 5 largest cities are Los Angeles, San Diego, San Jose, San Francisco, and Long Beach, with Los Angeles, San Diego, and San Jose each having at least 1 million residents. Like many populous states, California's capital, Sacramento is smaller than the state's largest city, Los Angeles. The state is home to the nation's 2nd- and 6th-largest census statistical areas and 8 of the nation's 50 most populous cities. California has a varied climate and geography and a multi-cultural population.

California's geography ranges from the Pacific Coast to the Sierra Nevada Mountains in the east, to the Mojave Desert areas in the southeast and the Redwood–Douglas fir forests of the northwest. The center of the state is dominated by the Central Valley, one of the most productive agricultural areas in the world. California is the most geographically diverse state in the nation, and contains the highest (Mount Whitney) and lowest (Death Valley) points in the contiguous United States. Almost 40% of California is forested, a high amount for a relatively arid state.

The name *California* once referred to a large area of North America, including much of the southwestern United States and the Baja California peninsula. Beginning in the late 18th century, the area known as Alta California (Upper California) (roughly speaking, what is now the southwestern USA west of the prairie) was colonized by the Spanish Empire, being part of the Viceroyalty of New Spain. In 1821, Mexico, including Alta California, became the First Mexican Empire, beginning as a monarchy, before shifting to a republic. In 1846 a group of American settlers in Sonoma declared the independence of a California Republic in Alta California. As a result of the Mexican-American War, Mexico ceded Alta California to the United States. Western areas of Alta California became the state of California, the 31st state admitted to the union on September 9, 1850, while eastern areas were assigned to various U.S. territories.

In the 19th century, the California Gold Rush brought about dramatic social, economic, and demographic change in California, with a large influx of people and an economic boom that caused San Francisco to grow from a hamlet of tents to a world-renowned boomtown. Key developments in the early 20th century included the emergence of Los Angeles as center of the American entertainment industry, and the growth of a large, state-wide tourism sector. In addition to California's prosperous agricultural industry, other important contributors to the economy include aerospace, petroleum, and information technology. If California were a country, it would rank among the ten largest economies in the world, with a GDP similar to that of Italy. It would be the 35th most populous country.

Etymology

Main article: Origin of the name California

The word *California* originally referred to the entire region composed of what is today the state of California, plus all or parts of Nevada, Utah, Arizona, and Wyoming, and the Mexican peninsula of Baja California.

The name *California* is most commonly believed to have derived from a fictional paradise peopled by Black Amazons and ruled by a Queen Califia. The myth of Califia is recorded in a 1510 work *The*

Exploits of Esplandian, written as a sequel to *Amadís de Gaula* by Spanish adventure writer Garci Rodríguez de Montalvo. The kingdom of Queen Califia or Calafia, according to Montalvo, was said to be a remote land inhabited by griffins and other strange beasts and rich in gold.

> Know ye that at the right hand of the Indies there is an island named California, very close to that part of the terrestrial Paradise, which was inhabited by black women, without a single man among them, and that they lived in the manner of Amazons. They were robust of body, with strong and passionate hearts and great virtues. The island itself is one of the wildest in the world on account of the bold and craggy rocks. Their weapons were all made of gold. The island everywhere abounds with gold and precious stones, and upon it no other metal was found.Wikipedia:Verifiability

The name *California* is the fifth-oldest surviving European place-name in the U.S. and was applied to what is now the southern tip of Baja California as the *island of California* by a Spanish expedition led by Diego de Becerra and Fortun Ximenez, who landed there in 1533 at the behest of Hernando Cortes.

Geography

Main article: Geography of California

California adjoins the Pacific Ocean, Oregon, Nevada, Arizona, and the Mexican state of Baja California. With an area of 160000 square miles (414000 km^2), it is the third-largest state in the United States in size, after Alaska and Texas. If it were a country, California would be the 59th-largest in the world in area.

In the middle of the state lies the California Central Valley, bounded by the coastal mountain ranges in the west, the Sierra Nevada to the east, the Cascade Range in the north and the Tehachapi Mountains in the south.

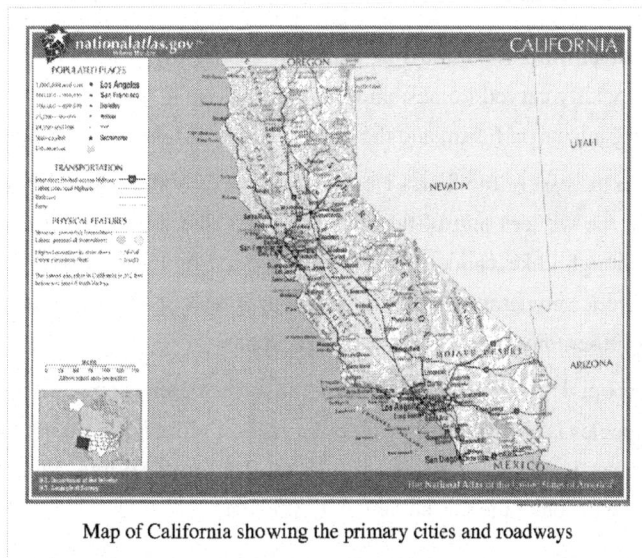
Map of California showing the primary cities and roadways

The Central Valley is California's agricultural heartland and grows approximately one-third of the nation's food.

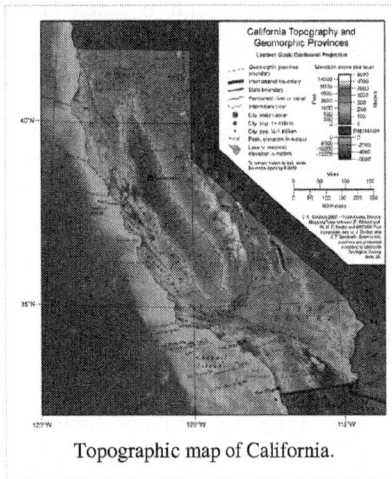
Topographic map of California.

Divided in two by the Sacramento-San Joaquin River Delta, the northern portion, the Sacramento Valley serves as the watershed of the Sacramento River, while the southern portion, the San Joaquin Valley is the watershed for the San Joaquin River; both areas derive their names from the rivers that transit them. With dredging, the Sacramento and the San Joaquin Rivers have remained sufficiently deep that several inland cities are seaports.

The Sacramento-San Joaquin River Delta serves as a critical water supply hub for the state. Water is routed through an extensive network of canals and pumps out of the delta, that traverse nearly the length of the state, including the Central Valley Project and the State Water Project. Water from the Delta provides drinking water for nearly 23 million people, almost two-thirds of the state's population, and provides water to farmers on the west side of the San Joaquin Valley. The Channel Islands are located off the southern coast.

The Sierra Nevada (Spanish for "snowy range") includes the highest peak in the contiguous forty-eight states, Mount Whitney, at 14,505 ft (4,421 m). The range embraces Yosemite Valley, famous for its glacially carved domes, and Sequoia National Park, home to the giant sequoia trees, the largest living organisms on Earth, and the deep freshwater lake, Lake Tahoe, the largest lake in the state by volume.

To the east of the Sierra Nevada are Owens Valley and Mono Lake, an essential migratory bird habitat. In the western part of the state is Clear Lake, the largest freshwater lake by area entirely in California. Though Lake Tahoe is larger, it is divided by the California/Nevada border. The Sierra Nevada falls to Arctic temperatures in winter and has several dozen small glaciers, including Palisade Glacier, the southernmost glacier in the United States.

About 45 percent of the state's total surface area is covered by forests, and California's diversity of pine species is unmatched by any other state. California contains more forestland than any other state except Alaska. Many of the trees in the California White Mountains are the oldest in the world; one Bristlecone pine has an age of 4,700 years.

In the south is a large inland salt lake, the Salton Sea. The south-central desert is called the Mojave; to the northeast of the Mojave lies Death Valley, which contains the lowest, hottest point in North America, Badwater Basin. The distance from the lowest point of Death Valley to the peak of Mount Whitney is less than 200 miles (322 km). Indeed, almost all of southeastern California is arid, hot desert, with routine extreme high temperatures during the summer. The southeastern border of California with Arizona is entirely formed by the Colorado River, from which the southern part of the state gets about half of its water.

Along the California coast are several major metropolitan areas, including Greater Los Angeles, the San Francisco Bay Area, and San Diego.

As part of the Ring of Fire, California is subject to tsunamis, floods, droughts, Santa Ana winds, wildfires, landslides on steep terrain, and has several volcanoes. It sees numerous earthquakes due to several faults, in particular the San Andreas Fault.

Climate

Main article: Climate of California

California's climate varies from Mediterranean to subarctic.

Much of the state has a Mediterranean climate, with cool, rainy winters and dry summers. The cool California Current offshore often creates summer fog near the coast. Further inland, one encounters colder winters and hotter summers.

Coastline at Big Sur.

Northern parts of the state average higher annual rainfall than the south. California's mountain ranges influence the climate as well: some of the rainiest parts of the state are west-facing mountain slopes. Northwestern California has a temperate climate, and the Central Valley has a Mediterranean climate but with greater temperature extremes than the coast. The high mountains, including the Sierra Nevada, have a mountain climate with snow in winter and mild to moderate heat in summer.

The east side of California's mountains produce a rain shadow, creating expansive deserts. The higher elevation deserts of eastern California see hot summers and cold winters, while the low deserts east of the southern California mountains experience hot summers and nearly frostless mild winters. Death Valley, a desert with large expanses below sea level, is considered the hottest location in North America; the highest temperature in the Western Hemisphere, 134 °F (57 °C), was recorded there on July 10, 1913.

Ecology

Main article: Ecology of California

California is one of the richest and most diverse parts of the world, and includes some of the most endangered ecological communities. California is part of the Nearctic ecozone and spans a number of terrestrial ecoregions.

California's large number of endemic species includes relict species, which have died out elsewhere, such as the Catalina Ironwood (*Lyonothamnus floribundus*). Many other endemics originated through differentiation or adaptive radiation, whereby multiple species develop from a common ancestor to take advantage of diverse ecological conditions such as the California lilac (*Ceanothus*). Many California endemics have become endangered, as urbanization, logging, overgrazing, and the introduction of exotic species have encroached on their habitat.

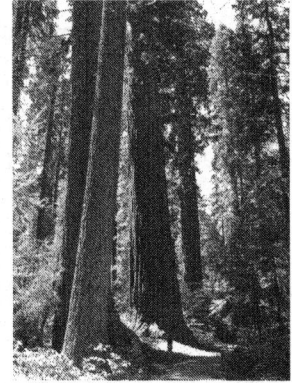
Calaveras Big Trees State Park

Flora and Fauna

California boasts several superlatives in its collection of flora: the largest trees, the tallest trees, and the oldest trees. California's native grasses are perennial plants. After European contact, these were generally replaced by invasive species of European annual grasses; and, in modern times, California's hills turn a characteristic golden-brown in summer.

Because California has the greatest diversity of climate and terrain, the state has six life zones which are the lower Sonoran (desert); upper Sonoran (foothill regions and some coastal lands), transition (coastal areas and moist northeastern counties); and the Canadian, Hudsonian, and Arctic Zones, comprising the state's highest elevations.

Plant life in the dry climate of the lower Sonoran zone contains a diversity of native cactus, mesquite, and paloverde. The Joshua tree (Yucca brevifolia) is found in the Mojave Desert. Flowering plants include the dward desert poppy and a variety of asters. Fremont cottonwood and valley oak thrive in the Central Valley. The upper Sonoran zone includes the chaparral belt, characterized by forests of small shrubs, stunted trees, and herbaceous plants. Nemophila, mint, phacelia, viola, and the golden poppy (Eschscholtzia californica)- the state flower- also flourish in this zone, along with the lupine, more species of which occur here than anywhere else in the world.

The transition zone includes most of California's forests with the redwood (Sequoia sempervirens) and the "big tree" or giant sequoia (Sequoia gigantea), among the oldest living things on earth (some are said to have lived at least 4,000 years). Tanbark oak, California laurel, sugar pine, madrona, broad-leaved maple, and Douglas fir also grow here. Forest floors are covered with swordfern, alumnroot, barrenwort, and trillium, and there are tickets of huckleberry, azalea, elder, and wild currant. Characteristic wild flowers include varieties of mariposa, tulip, and tiger and leopard lilies.

The high elevations of the Canadian zone allow the Jeffrey pine, red fir, and lodgepole pine to thrive. Brushy areas are abundant with dwarf manzanita and ceanothus; the unique Sierra puffball is also found here. Right below the timeberline, in the Hudsonian zone, the whitebark, foxtail, and silver pines grow. At about 10,500 ft (3,200 m), begins the Arctic zone, a treeless region whose flora include a number of wildflowers, including Sierra primrose, yellow columbine, alpine buttercup, and alpine shooting star.

Common plants that have been introduced to the state include the eucalyptus, acacia, pepper tree, geranium, and Scotch broom. The species that are federally classified as endangered are the Contra Costa wallflower, Antioch Dunes evening primrose, Solano Grass, San Clemente Island larkspur, salt marsh bird's beak, McDonald's rock-cress, and Santa Barbara Island Liveforever. As of December 1997, eight-five plant species were listed as threatened or endangered.

In the deserts of the lower Sonoran zone, the mammals include the jackrabbit, kangaroo rat, squirrel, and opossum. Common birds include the night owl, roadrunner, cactus wren, a various species of hawk. The area's reptilian life include the sidewinder viper, desert tortoise, and horned toad. The upper Sonoran zone boasts mammals such as the antelope, brown-footed woodrat, and ring-tailed cat. Birds unique to this zone are the California thrasher, bush tit, and California condor.

In the transition zone, there are Colombian black-tailed deer, black bear, gray fox, cougar, bobcat, and Roosevelt elk. Reptiles such as the garter snakes and rattlesnakes inhabit the zone. In addition, amphibians such as the water puppy and redwood salamander are common too. Birds such as the kingfisher, chickadee, towhee, and hummingbird thrive here as well.

The Canadian zone mammals include the mountain weasel, snowshoe hare, Sierra chickadee, and several species of chipmunks. Conspicuous birds include the blue-fronted jay, Sierra hermit thrush, water ouzel, and Townsend solitaire. As one ascends into the Hudsonian zone, birds become scarcer. While the Sierra rosy finch is the only bird native to the high Arctic region, other bird species such as the hummingbird and Clark nutcracker. Principal mammals found in this region include the Sierra coney, white-tailed jackrabbit, and the bighorn sheep. As of April 2003, the bighorn sheep was listed as endangered by the US Fish and Wildlife Service. The fauna found throughout several zones are the mule deer, coyote, mountain lion, red-shafted flicker, and several species of hawk and sparrow.

Aquatic life in California thrives, from the state's mountain lakes and streams to the rocky Pacific coastline. Numerous trout species are found, among them rainbow, golden, and Tahoe. Migratory species of salmon are common as well. Deep-sea life forms include sea bass, yellowfin tuna, barracuda, and several types of whale. Native to the cliffs of northern California are seals, sea lions, and many types of shorebirds, including migratory species.

As of April 2003, 118 California animals were on the federal endangered list; 181 plants were listed as endangered or threatened. Endangered animals include the San Joaquin kitfox, Point Arena mountain beaver, Pacific pocket mouse, salt marsh harvest mouse, Morro Bay kangaroo rat (and five other species of kangaroo rat), Amargosa vole, California least tern, California condor, San Clemente loggerhead shrike, San Clemente sage sparrow, San Francisco garter snake, five species of salamander, three species of chub, and two species of pupfish. Eleven butterflies are also endangered and two that are threatened are on the federal list. Among threatened animals are the coastal California gnatcatcher, Paiute cutthroat trout, southern sea otter, and northern spotted owl. California has a total of

290821 acres (1176.91 km^2) of National Wildlife Refuges. As of September 2010, 123 California animals were listed as either endangered or threatened on the federal list provided by the US Fish & Wildlife Service. Also, as of the same year, 178 species of California plants were listed either as endangered or threatened on this federal list.

Rivers

Main article: List of California rivers

The most prominent rivers within California are the Sacramento River, the Pit River and the San Joaquin River, which drain the Central Valley and the west slope of the Sierra Nevada and flow to the Pacific Ocean through San Francisco Bay. Some other important rivers are the Klamath River and the Trinity River, in the north, and the Colorado River, on the southeast border.

The Owens River takes runoff from the southeastern slopes of the Sierra Nevada and flows into Owens Lake. The Eel River and Salinas River each drain portions of the California coast, north and south of San Francisco Bay, respectively. The Mojave River is the primary watercourse in the Mojave Desert and the Santa Ana River drains much of the Transverse Ranges and bisects Southern California.

Regions

Main article: List of regions of California

Mount Whitney, the highest point in the Contiguous United States

- Central Valley
- Coastal California
- Northern California
  - Central California
  - San Francisco Bay Area
  - Sierra Nevada
  - Upstate California
- Eastern California
  - Inland Empire (Also included in Southern California)
- Southern California
  - Greater Los Angeles
  - Inland Empire (Also included in Eastern California)
  - Border Region

History

History of California
This article is part of **a series**
Timeline
To 1899
Gold Rush (1848)
US Civil War (1861-1865)
Since 1900
Topics
Maritime · Railroad ·
Highways · Slavery
Cities
Los Angeles · Sacramento ·
San Diego · San Jose · Visalia
California Portal

Main article: History of California

Settled by successive waves of arrivals during the last 10,000 years, California was one of the most culturally and linguistically diverse areas in pre-Columbian North America; The Indigenous peoples of California included more than 70 distinct groups of Native Americans. Large, settled populations lived on the coast and hunted sea mammals, fished for salmon and gathered shellfish; groups in the interior hunted terrestrial game, and gathered nuts, acorns and berries. California groups also were diverse in their political organization with bands, tribes, villages, and on the resource-rich coasts, large chiefdoms, such as the Chumash, Pomo and Salinan. Trade, intermarriage and military alliances fostered many social and economic relationships among the diverse groups.

The first European to explore the coast as far north as the Russian River was the Portuguese João Rodrigues Cabrilho, in 1542, sailing for the Spanish Empire. Some 37 years later English explorer Francis Drake also explored and claimed an undefined portion of the California coast in 1579. Spanish traders made unintended visits with the Manila Galleons on their return trips from the Philippines beginning in 1565. Sebastián Vizcaíno explored and mapped the coast of California in 1602 for New Spain.

Spanish missionaries began setting up 21 California Missions along the coast of what became known as Alta California (Upper California), together with small towns and *presidios*. In 1821 the Mexican War of Independence gave Mexico (including California) independence from Spain; for the next 25 years, Alta California remained a remote northern province of the nation of Mexico. Cattle ranches, or *ranchos*, emerged as the dominant institutions of Mexican California. After Mexican independence from Spain, the chain of missions became the property of the Mexican government and were secularized by 1832. The ranchos developed under ownership by Californios (Spanish-speaking Californians) who had received land grants, and traded cowhides and tallow with Boston merchants.

Beginning in the 1820s, trappers and settlers from the U.S. and Canada began to arrive in Northern California, harbingers of the great changes that would later sweep the Mexican territory. These new arrivals used the Siskiyou Trail, California Trail, Oregon Trail and Old Spanish Trail to cross the rugged mountains and harsh deserts surrounding California. In this period, Imperial Russia explored the California coast and established a trading post at Fort Ross.

In 1846 settlers rebelled against Mexican rule during the Bear Flag Revolt. Afterwards, rebels raised the Bear Flag (featuring a bear, a star, a red stripe and the words "California Republic") at Sonoma.

The Bear Flag of the Republic of California

> "[We] overthrow a Government which has seized upon the property of the Missions for its individual aggrandizement; which has ruined and shamefully oppressed the laboring people of California."

—William Ide, Declaration from the Bear Flag Revolt

The Republic's first and only president was William B. Ide, who played a pivotal role during the Bear Flag Revolt. His term lasted 22 days and concluded when California was occupied by U.S. forces during the Mexican-American War.

The California Republic was short lived. The same year marked the outbreak of the Mexican-American War (1846–1848). When Commodore John D. Sloat of the United States Navy sailed into Monterey Bay and began the military occupation of California by the United States. Northern California capitulated in less than a month to the U.S. forces. After a series of defensive battles in Southern California, including The Siege of Los Angeles, the Battle of Dominguez Rancho, the Battle of San Pasqual, the Battle of Rio San Gabriel and the Battle of La Mesa, the Treaty of Cahuenga was signed by the Californios on January 13, 1847, securing American control in California. Following the Treaty of Guadalupe Hidalgo that ended the war, the region was divided between Mexico and the U.S.; the western territory of Alta California, was to become the U.S. state of California, and Arizona, Nevada,

Colorado and Utah became U.S. Territories, while the lower region of California, Baja California, remained in the possession of Mexico.

San Francisco harbor c. 1850. Between 1847 and 1870, the population of San Francisco increased from 500 to 150,000.

In 1848 the non-native population of California was estimated to be no more than 15,000. But after gold was discovered, the population burgeoned with U.S. citizens, Europeans and other immigrants during the great California Gold Rush. By 1854 over 300,000 settlers had come. On September 9, 1850, as part of the Compromise of 1850, California was admitted to the United States as a free state (one in which slavery was prohibited).

The seat of government for California under Mexican rule was located at Monterey from 1777 until 1835, when Mexican authorities abandoned California, leaving their missions and military forts behind. In 1849 the Constitutional Convention was first held there. Among the duties was the task of determining the location for the new state capital. The first legislative sessions were held in San Jose (1850–1851). Subsequent locations included Vallejo (1852–1853), and nearby Benicia (1853–1854); these locations eventually proved to be inadequate as well. The capital has been located in Sacramento since 1854 with only a short break in 1861 when legislative sessions were held in San Francisco due to flooding in Sacramento.

Travel between California and the central and eastern parts of the U.S. was time consuming and dangerous. A more direct connection came in 1869 with the completion of the First Transcontinental Railroad through Donner Pass in the Sierra Nevada mountains. After this rail link was established, hundreds of thousands of U.S. citizens came west, where new Californians were discovering that land in the state, if irrigated during the dry summer months, was extremely well-suited to fruit cultivation and agriculture in general. Vast expanses of wheat, other cereal crops, vegetable crops, cotton, and nut and fruit trees were grown (including oranges in Southern California), and the foundation was laid for the state's prodigious agricultural production in the Central Valley and elsewhere.

The intersection of Hollywood Boulevard and Highland Avenue in Hollywood 1907. In less than two decades, Hollywood would become an international center of the entertainment industry.

During the early-20th century, migration to California accelerated with the completion of major transcontinental highways like the Lincoln Highway and Route 66. In the period from 1900 to 1965 the population grew from fewer than one million to become the most populous state in the Union. The state is regarded as a world center of technology and engineering businesses, of the entertainment and music industries, and as the U.S. center of agricultural production.

Demographics

Main article: Demographics of California

Population

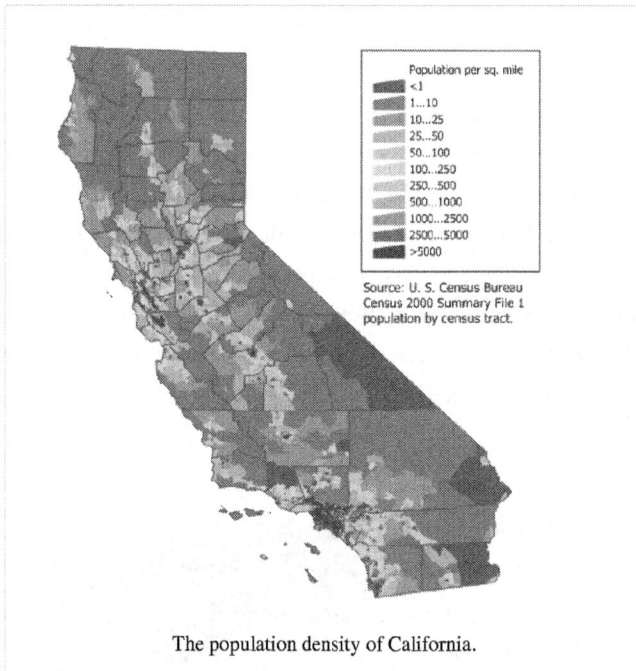

Source: U. S. Census Bureau
Census 2000 Summary File 1
population by census tract.

The population density of California.

Historical populations		
Census	Pop.	%±
1850	92597	—
1860	379994	310.4%
1870	560247	47.4%
1880	864694	54.3%
1890	1213398	40.3%
1900	1485053	22.4%
1910	2377549	60.1%

1920	3426861	44.1%
1930	5677251	65.7%
1940	6907387	21.7%
1950	10586223	53.3%
1960	15717204	48.5%
1970	19953134	27.0%
1980	23667902	18.6%
1990	29760021	25.7%
2000	33871648	13.8%
Est. 2009	36961664	9.1%

California's population is estimated by the US Census Bureau at 36,961,664 for the year 2009, making it the most populous state. This includes a natural increase of 3,090,016 since the last census (5,058,440 births minus 2,179,958 deaths). During this time period, international migration produced a net increase of 1,816,633 people while domestic migration produced a net decrease of 1,509,708, resulting in a net in-migration of 306,925 people. The State of California's own statistics show a population of 38,292,687 for January 1, 2009.

California is the second-most-populous sub-national entity of the Western Hemisphere, exceeded only by the State of São Paulo, Brazil.Wikipedia:No original research#Synthesis of published material that advances a positionWikipedia:Identifying reliable sources California's population is greater than that of all but 34 countries of the world. Also, Los Angeles County has held the title of most populous U.S. county for decades, and it alone is more populous than 42 U.S. states. The center of population of California is located in the town of Buttonwillow, Kern County.

In 2010, illegal immigrants constituted an estimated 7.3 percent of the population. This was the third highest percentage of any state in the country.

Starting in the year 2010, for the first time since the California Gold Rush, California-born residents make up the majority of the state's population.

Cities

California is home to eight of the 50 most populous cities in the United States.

Racial and ancestral makeup

According to the 2006–2008 American Community Survey, California's population is:

- 42.3% White (not including White Hispanic)
- 36.6% are Hispanic or Latino (of any race)
- 12.5% Asian
- 6.7% Black or African American
- 2.6% Multiracial
- 1.2% Native American

With regard to demographics, California has the largest population of White Americans in the U.S., an estimated 22,189,514 residents, although most demographic surveys do not measure actual genetic ancestry. The state has the fifth-largest population of African Americans in the U.S., an estimated 2,250,630 residents. California's Asian American population is estimated at 4.4 million, approximately one-third of the nation's 13.1 million Asian Americans. California's Native American population of 285,162 is the most of any state.

According to estimates from 2008, California has the largest minority population in the United States by numbers, making up 57% of the state population. In 2000, Hispanics comprised 32% of the population; that number grew to 37% in 2008. Non-Hispanic whites decreased from 80% of the state's population in 1970 to 42% in 2008. While the population of minorities account for 102 million of 301 million U.S. residents, 20% of the national total live in California.

Armed forces

As of 2002, the US Department of Defense had Wikipedia:Identifying reliable sources

- 123,948 active-duty military personnel
    - 7,932 US Army personnel
    - 96,047 US Navy (including 20,000+US Marines)
    - 19,969 Air Force
- 58,076 DOD civilian personnel

As of 2000 there were 2,569,340 veterans of US military service: 504,010 served in World War II, 301,034 in the Korean conflict, 754,682 during the Vietnam era, and 278,003 during 1990–2000 (including the Persian Gulf War).

California's military forces consist of the Army and Air National Guard, the naval and state military reserve (militia), and the California Cadet Corps.

Languages

As of 2005, 57.59% of California residents age five and older spoke English as a first language at home, while 28.21% spoke Spanish. In addition to English and Spanish, 2.04% spoke Filipino, 1.59% spoke Chinese (which included Cantonese [0.63%] and Mandarin [0.43%]), 1.4% spoke Vietnamese, and 1.05% spoke Korean as their mother tongue. In total, 42.4% of the population spoke languages other than English. California is viewed as one of the most linguistically diverse areas in the world (the indigenous languages were derived from 64 root languages in 6 language families). About half of the indigenous languages are no longer spoken, and all of California's living indigenous languages are endangered and there are some efforts toward language revitalization.Wikipedia:Avoid weasel words

The official language of California has been English since the passage of Proposition 63 in 1986. However, many state, city, and local government agencies still continue to print official public documents in numerous languages.

Culture

Main article: Culture of California

The culture of California is a Western culture and most clearly has its modern roots in the culture of the United States, but also, historically, many Hispanic influences. As a border and coastal state, Californian culture has been greatly influenced by several large immigrant populations, especially those from Latin America. California is a true melting pot as well as an international crossroad to the U.S.

California has long been a subject of interest in the public mind and has often been promoted by its boosters as a kind of paradise. In the early 20th Century, fueled by the efforts of state and local boosters, many Americans saw the Golden State as an ideal resort destination, sunny and dry all year round with easy access to the ocean and mountains. In the 1960s, popular music groups such as the Beach Boys promoted the image of Californians as laid-back, tanned beach-goers.

In terms of socio-cultural mores and national politics, Californians are perceived as more liberal than other Americans, especially those who live in the inland states. In some ways, California is the quintessential Blue State-- accepting of alternative lifestyles, not uniformly religious, and preoccupied with environmental issues.

The gold rush of the 1850s is still seen as a symbol of California's economic style, which tends to generate technology, social, entertainment, and economic fads and booms and related busts.

Religion

The largest religious denominations by number of adherents as a percentage of California's population in 2008 were the Roman Catholic Church with 31 percent; Evangelical Protestants with 18 percent; and Mainline Protestants with 14 percent. Those unaffiliated with any religion represented 21 percent of the population.

Cathedral Basilica of St. Joseph in San Jose

There are approximately 1 million Muslims in California, which is the largest population of any U.S. state. They are mainly of African American descent and a large Middle-Eastern immigrant population.Wikipedia:No original research#Synthesis of published material that advances a position The Federal Bureau of Investigation estimates that approximately 100,000 Muslims reside in San Diego.

As the twentieth century came to a close, forty percent of all Buddhists in America resided in Southern California. The Los Angeles Metropolitan Area has become unique in the Buddhist world as the only place where representative organizations of every major school of Buddhism can be found in a single urban center.Wikipedia:Verifiability The

Mission San Diego

City of Ten Thousand Buddhas in Northern California and Hsi Lai Temple in Southern California are two of the largest Buddhist temples in the Western Hemisphere.

The first priests to come to California were Roman Catholic missionaries from Spain. Roman Catholics founded 21 missions along the California coast, as well as the cities of Los Angeles and San Francisco. California continues to have a large Roman Catholic population due to the large numbers of Mexicans and Central Americans living within its borders. California has twelve dioceses and two archdioceses, the Archdiocese of Los Angeles and the Archdiocese of San Francisco, the former being the largest archdiocese in the United States.

With almost one million Jews, California has the highest number of Jews of any state except New York. Many of these Jews live in the West Los Angeles and San Fernando Valley regions of Los Angeles. At the present time, both of California's Senators, Dianne Feinstein and Barbara Boxer, are Jewish.

California has more members of The Church of Jesus Christ of Latter-day Saints and Temples than any state except Utah. Latter-day Saints (Mormons) have played important roles in the settlement of California throughout the state's history. For example, a group of a few hundred Mormon converts from the Northeastern United States and Europe arrived at what would become San Francisco in the 1840s aboard the ship *Brooklyn*, more than doubling the population of the small town. A group of Mormons also established the city of San Bernardino in Southern California in 1851. According to the LDS Church 2009 statistics, just over 750,000 Mormons reside in the state of California, attending almost 1400 congregations statewide.

However, a Pew Research Center survey revealed that California is somewhat less religious than the rest of the US: 62 percent of Californians say they are "absolutely certain" of the belief in God, while in the nation 71 percent say so. The survey also revealed 48 percent of Californians say religion is "very important," compared to 56 percent nationally.

Economy

Main article: Economy of California

As of 2007, the gross state product (GSP) is about $1.812 trillion, the largest in the United States. California is responsible for 13 percent of the United States gross domestic product (GDP). As of 2006, California's GDP is larger than all but eight countries in the world (all but eleven countries by Purchasing Power Parity). California's unemployment rate exceeds 12%.

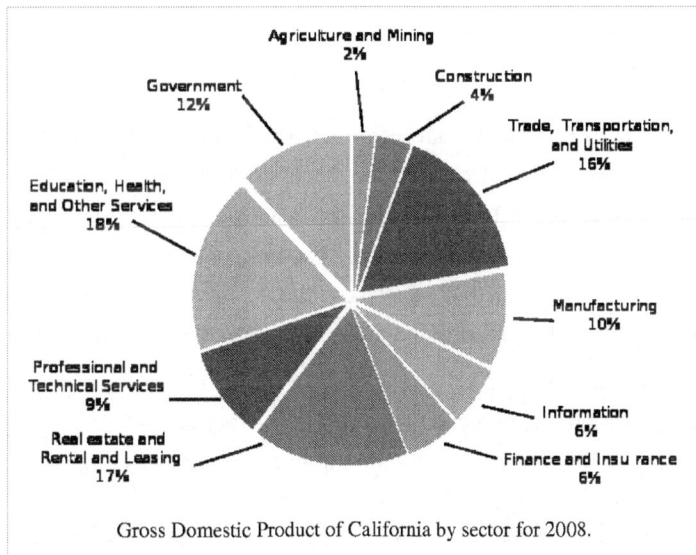

Gross Domestic Product of California by sector for 2008.

In terms of jobs, the five largest sectors in California are trade, transportation, and utilities; government; professional and business services; education and health services; and leisure and hospitality. In terms of output, the five largest sectors are financial services, followed by trade, transportation, and utilities; education and health services; government; and manufacturing.

California currently has the 5th highest unemployment rate in the nation at 12.5% as of January 2010 and had continued to rise, up significantly from 5.9% in 2007.

California's economy is very dependent on trade and international related commerce accounts for approximately one-quarter of the state's

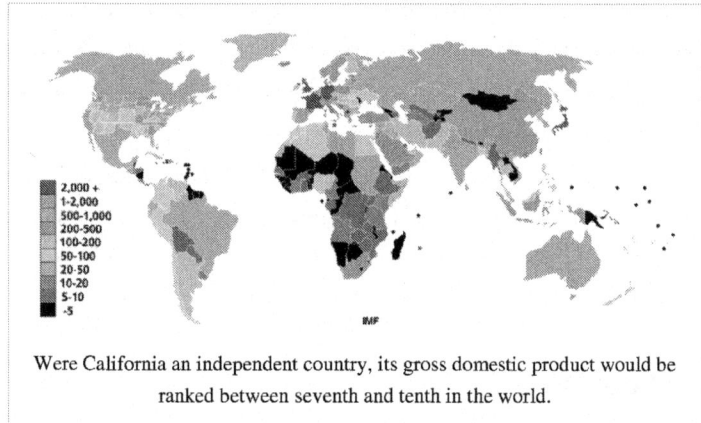

Were California an independent country, its gross domestic product would be ranked between seventh and tenth in the world.

economy. In 2008, California exported $144 billion worth of goods, up from $134 billion in 2007 and $127 billion in 2006. Computers and electronic products are California's top export, accounting for 42 percent of all the state's exports in 2008.

Agriculture is an important sector in California's economy. Farming-related sales more than quadrupled over the past three decades, from $7.3 billion in 1974 to nearly $31 billion in 2004. This increase has occurred despite a 15 percent decline in acreage devoted to farming during the period, and water supply suffering from chronic instability. Factors contributing to the growth in sales-per-acre include more intensive use of active farmlands and technological improvements in crop production.. In 2008, California's 81,500 farms and ranches generated $36.2 billion products revenue.

Per capita GDP in 2007 was $38,956, ranking eleventh in the nation. Per capita income varies widely by geographic region and profession. The Central Valley is the most impoverished, with migrant farm workers making less than minimum wage. Recently, the San Joaquin Valley was characterized as one of the most economically depressed regions in the U.S., on par with the region of Appalachia. Many coastal cities include some of the wealthiest per-capita areas in the U.S. The high-technology sectors in Northern California, specifically Silicon Valley, in Santa Clara and San Mateo counties, have emerged from the economic downturn caused by the dot-com bust.

In 2010, there were more than 663,000 millionaires in the state, more than any other state in the nation.

State finances

See also: 2008–10 California budget crisis

California levies a 9.3 percent maximum variable rate income tax, with six tax brackets, collecting about $40 billion per year (representing approximately 51% of General Fund revenue and 40% of tax revenue overall in FY2007). California has a state sales tax of 8.25%, which can total up to 10.75% with local sales tax included. All real property is taxable annually, the tax based on the property's fair market value at the time of purchase or completion of new construction. Property tax increases are capped at 2% per year (see Proposition 13).

However, California is facing a $26.3 billion budget deficit for the 2009–2010 budget year. While the legislative bodies appeared to address the problem in 2008 with the three-month delayed passage of a budget they in fact only postponed the deficit to 2009 and due to the late 2008 decline in the economy and the credit crisis the problem became urgent in November 2008.

One potential problem is that a substantial portion of the state's income comes from income taxes on a small proportion of wealthy citizens. For example, it is estimated that in 2004 the richest 3% of state taxpayers (those with tax returns showing over 200K USD yearly income) paid approximately 60% of state income taxes. The taxable income of this population is highly dependent upon capital gains, which has been severely impacted by the stock market declines of this period. The governor has proposed a combination of extensive program cuts and tax increases to address this problem, but owing to longstanding problems in the legislature these proposals are likely to be difficult to pass as legislation.

State spending increased from $56 billion in 1998 to $131 billion in 2008, and the state was facing a budget deficit of $40 billion in 2008. California is facing another budget gap for 2010, with $72 billion in debt.

In 2009 the California economic crisis became severe as the state faced insolvency.#obsolete In June 2009 Gov. Arnold Schwarzenegger said "Our wallet is empty, our bank is closed and our credit is dried up." He called for massive budget cuts of $24 billion, about $\frac{1}{4}$ of the state's budget.

Energy

Main article: Energy use in California

Due to its mild weather and strong environmental movement, its *per capita* energy use is one of the smallest of any U.S. state.

In 1984, the Davis City Council declared the city to be a nuclear free zone. California voters banned the approval of new nuclear power plants since the late 1970s because of concerns over radioactive waste disposal.

Transportation

Main article: Transportation of California

California's vast terrain is connected by an extensive system of freeways, expressways, and highways. California is known for its car culture, giving California's cities a reputation for severe traffic congestion. Construction and maintenance of state roads and statewide transportation planning are primarily the responsibility of the California Department of Transportation (Caltrans). The rapidly growing population of the state is straining all of its transportation networks, and a recurring issue in California politics is whether the state should

The Golden Gate Bridge in San Francisco, one of California's most famous landmarks.

continue to aggressively expand its freeway network or concentrate on improving mass transit networks in urban areas.

One of the state's more visible landmarks, the Golden Gate Bridge was completed in 1937. With its orange paint and panoramic views of the bay, this highway bridge is a popular tourist attraction and also accommodates pedestrians and bicyclists. It is simultaneously designated as U.S. Route 101, which is part of the El Camino Real (Spanish for Royal Road or King's Highway), and State Route 1, also known as the Pacific Coast Highway. Another of the seven bridges in the San Francisco Bay Area is the San Francisco – Oakland Bay Bridge, completed in 1936. This bridge transports approximately 280,000 vehicles per day on two-decks, with its two sections meeting at Yerba Buena Island.

Los Angeles International Airport and San Francisco International Airport are major hubs for trans-Pacific and transcontinental traffic. There are about a dozen important commercial airports and many more general aviation airports throughout the state.

California also has several important seaports. The giant seaport complex formed by the Port of Los Angeles and the Port of Long Beach in Southern California is the largest in the country and responsible for handling about a fourth of all container cargo traffic in the United States. The Port of Oakland, fourth largest in the nation, handles trade from the Pacific Rim and delivers most of the ocean containers passing through Northern California to the entire USA.

Intercity rail travel is provided by Amtrak California, which manages the three busiest intercity rail lines in the US outside the Northeast Corridor. Integrated subway and light rail networks are found in Los Angeles (Metro Rail) and San Francisco (MUNI Metro). Light rail systems are also found in San Jose (VTA), San Diego (San Diego Trolley), Sacramento

Caltrans builds tall "stack" interchanges with soaring ramps that offer impressive views.

(RT Light Rail), and Northern San Diego County (Sprinter). Furthermore, commuter rail networks serve the San Francisco Bay Area (ACE, BART, Caltrain), Greater Los Angeles (Metrolink), and San Diego County (Coaster).

The California High Speed Rail Authority was created in 1996 by the state to implement an extensive 700 mile (1127 km) rail system. Construction was approved by the voters during the November 2008 general election, a $9.95 billion state bond will go toward its construction. Nearly all counties operate bus lines, and many cities operate their own bus lines as well. Intercity bus travel is provided by Greyhound and Amtrak Thruway Coach.

Government and politics

State government

Main article: Government of California

California is governed as a republic, with three branches of government — the executive branch consisting of the Governor and the other independently elected constitutional officers; the legislative branch consisting of the Assembly and Senate; and the judicial branch consisting of the Supreme Court of California and lower courts. The state also allows direct participation of the electorate by initiative, referendum, recall, and ratification. California allows each political party to choose whether to have a closed primary or a primary where only party members and independents vote. The state's capital is Sacramento.

The California State Capitol building in Sacramento.

The Governor of California and the other state constitutional officers serve four-year terms and may be re-elected only once. The California State Legislature consists of a 40-member Senate and 80-member Assembly. Senators serve four-year terms and Assembly members two. Members of the Assembly are subject to term limits of three terms, and members of the Senate are subject to term limits of two terms.

In the 2007–2008 session, there were 48 Democrats and 32 Republicans in the Assembly. In the Senate, there are 25 Democrats and 15 Republicans. The governor is Republican Arnold Schwarzenegger.

California's legal system is explicitly based upon English common law (as is the case with all other states except Louisiana) but carries a few features from Spanish civil law, such as community property. Capital punishment is a legal form of punishment and the state has the largest "Death Row" population in the country (though Texas is far more active in carrying out executions). California's "Death Row" is in San Quentin State Prison situated north of San Francisco in Marin County. Executions in California are currently on hold indefinitely as human rights issues are addressed. The number of inmates in California prisons has soared from 25,000 in 1980 to over 170,000 in 2007.

California's judiciary is the largest in the United States (with a total of 1,600 judges, while the federal system has only about 840). It is supervised by the seven Justices of the Supreme Court of California. Justices of the Supreme Court and Courts of Appeal are appointed by the Governor, but are subject to retention by the electorate every 12 years.

Federal politics

Main article: Politics of California

Presidential elections results

Year	Republican	Democratic
2008	36.91% 5,011,781	**60.94% 8,274,473**
2004	44.36% 5,509,826	**54.40% 6,745,485**
2000	41.65% 4,567,429	**53.45% 5,861,203**
1996	38.21% 3,828,380	**51.10% 5,119,835**
1992	32.61% 3,630,574	**46.01% 5,121,325**
1988	**51.13% 5,054,917**	47.56% 4,702,233
1984	**57.51% 5,467,009**	41.27% 3,922,519
1980	**52.69% 4,524,858**	35.91% 3,083,661
1976	**49.35% 3,882,244**	47.57% 3,742,284
1972	**55.01% 4,602,096**	41.54% 3,475,847
1968	**47.82% 3,467,664**	44.74% 3,244,318
1964	40.79% 2,879,108	**59.11% 4,171,877**
1960	**50.10% 3,259,722**	49.55% 3,224,099

California has an idiosyncratic political culture. It was the second state to legalize abortion and the second state to legalize marriage for gay couples (by judicial review, which was later revoked by the ballot initiative, Proposition 8).

Since 1990, California has generally elected Democratic candidates; however, the state has elected Republican Governors, though many of its Republican Governors, such as Governor Schwarzenegger, tend to be considered "Moderate Republicans" and more centrist than the national party.

Democratic strength is centered in coastal regions of Los Angeles County and the San Francisco Bay Area. The Democrats also hold a majority in Sacramento. Republican strength is greatest in eastern parts of the state. Orange County also remains mostly Republican.

California politics has trended towards the Democratic Party and away from the Republican Party. The trend is most obvious in presidential elections. Additionally, the Democrats have easily won every U.S. Senate race since 1992 and have maintained consistent majorities in both houses of the state legislature. In the U.S. House, the Democrats hold a 34–19 edge for the 110th United States Congress.

The U.S senators are Dianne Feinstein (D), a native of San Francisco, and Barbara Boxer (D). The districts in California are usually dominated by one or the other party with very few districts that could be considered competitive. Once very conservative having elected Republicans, California is now a reliable Democratic state. According to political analysts, California should soon gain three more seats, for a total of 58 electoral votes – the most electoral votes in the nation.

Cities, towns and counties

For lists of cities, towns, and counties in California, see List of counties in California, List of cities in California (by population), List of cities in California, List of urbanized areas in California (by population), and California locations by per capita income.

The state's local government is divided into 58 counties and 481 incorporated cities and towns; of which 459 are cities and 22 are towns. Under California law, the terms "city" and "town" are explicitly interchangeable; the name of an incorporated municipality in the state can either be "City of (Name)" or "Town of (Name)".

Sacramento became California's first incorporated city on February 27, 1850. San Jose, San Diego and Benicia tied for California's second incorporated city, each receiving incorporation on March 27, 1850. Eastvale became the state's most recent and 481st incorporated municipality on October 1, 2010.

The majority of these cities and towns are within one of five metropolitan areas. Sixty-eight percent of California's population lives in its three largest metropolitan areas, Greater Los Angeles, the San Francisco Bay Area, and the Riverside-San Bernardino Area (Inland Empire). Although smaller, the other two large population centers are the San Diego and the Sacramento metro areas.

The state recognizes two kinds of cities: charter and general law. General law cities owe their existence to state law and are consequentially governed by it; charter cities are governed by their own city charters. Cities incorporated in the 19th century tend to be charter cities. All ten of the state's most populous cities are charter cities.

Education

Main article: Education in California

See also: List of colleges and universities in California

Public secondary education consists of high schools that teach elective courses in trades, languages, and liberal arts with tracks for gifted, college-bound and industrial arts students. California's public educational system is supported by a unique constitutional amendment that requires a minimum annual funding level for grades K-12 and community colleges that grows with the economy and student enrollment figures.

Torrance High School is one of the oldest high schools in continuous use in California and a popular location for television and motion picture production.

California had over 6.2 million school students in the 2005–06 school year. Funding and staffing levels in California schools lag behind other states. In expenditure per pupil, California ranked 29th (of the 50 states and the District of Columbia) in 2005–06. In teaching staff expenditure per pupil, California ranked 49th of 51. In overall teacher-pupil ratio, California was also 49th, with 21 students per teacher. Only Arizona and Utah were lower.

California's public postsecondary education offers a unique three tiered system:

- The research university system in the state is the University of California (UC), a public university system. There are ten general UC campuses, and a number of specialized campuses in the UC system.
- The California State University (CSU) system has almost 450,000 students, making it the largest university system in the United States. It is intended to accept the top one-third of high school students. The 23 CSU schools are primarily intended for undergraduate education.
- The California Community Colleges system provides lower division coursework as well as basic skills and workforce training. It is the largest network of higher education in the US, composed of 110 colleges serving a student population of over 2.9 million.

California is also home to such notable private universities as Stanford University, the University of Southern California, the California Institute of Technology, and the Claremont Colleges. California has hundreds of other private colleges and universities, including many religious and special-purpose institutions.

Sports

Main articles: Sports in California and List of professional sports teams in California

California hosted the 1960 Winter Olympics at Squaw Valley Ski Resort, the 1932 and 1984 Summer Olympics in Los Angeles, as well as the 1994 FIFA World Cup.

California has nineteen major professional sports league franchises, far more than any other state. The San Francisco Bay Area has seven major league teams spread in three cities, San Francisco, Oakland and San Jose. While the Greater Los Angeles Area is home to ten major league franchises, it is also the largest metropolitan area not to have a team from the National Football League. San Diego has two major league teams, and Sacramento also has two.

Home to some of the most prominent universities in the United States, California has long had many respected collegiate sports programs. California home to the oldest college bowl game, the annual Rose Bowl, among others.

Los Angeles Memorial Coliseum, the only stadium in the world to host the Olympic Games twice: in 1932 and 1984

California has also long been a hub for motorsports and auto racing. The city of Long Beach holds an event every year in the month of April, which is host to IRL IndyCar Series racing through the streets of downtown. Long Beach has hosted Formula One events there in the past, and also currently hosts an event on the American Le Mans Series schedule. Auto Club Speedway is a speedway in Fontana, and currently hosts one to two NASCAR Sprint Cup Series races a year, and used to host CART Indycar races. Infineon Raceway in Sonoma is a multi-purpose facility, featuring a road course and a drag strip. The road course is home to a NASCAR event, an IRL Indycar event, and used to host an International Motor Sports Association sports car event. The drag strip hosts a yearly NHRA event. Mazda Raceway Laguna Seca is a roadcourse that currently hosts an ALMS event, and formerly hosted CART events. And Auto Club Raceway at Pomona has hosted NHRA drag racing for over 50 years now.

Below is a list of major sports teams in California:

Club	Sport	League
Oakland Raiders	American football	National Football League
San Diego Chargers	American football	National Football League
San Francisco 49ers	American football	National Football League
Sacramento Mountain Lions	American football	United Football League
Los Angeles Dodgers	Baseball	Major League Baseball
Los Angeles Angels of Anaheim	Baseball	Major League Baseball
Oakland Athletics	Baseball	Major League Baseball
San Diego Padres	Baseball	Major League Baseball
San Francisco Giants	Baseball	Major League Baseball
Golden State Warriors	Basketball	National Basketball Association
Los Angeles Clippers	Basketball	National Basketball Association
Los Angeles Lakers	Basketball	National Basketball Association
Sacramento Kings	Basketball	National Basketball Association
Anaheim Ducks	Ice hockey	National Hockey League
Los Angeles Kings	Ice hockey	National Hockey League
San Jose Sharks	Ice hockey	National Hockey League
Chivas USA	Soccer	Major League Soccer
Los Angeles Galaxy	Soccer	Major League Soccer
San Jose Earthquakes	Soccer	Major League Soccer
Los Angeles Sparks	Basketball	Women's National Basketball Association
Stockton Cougars	Soccer	Professional Arena Soccer League
FC Gold Pride	Soccer	Women's Professional Soccer

See also

Main articles: Outline of California and Index of California-related articles

Further reading

- Chartkoff, Joseph L.; Chartkoff, Kerry Kona (1984). *The archaeology of California*. Stanford: Stanford University Press. ISBN 0804711577. OCLC 11351549 [1].
- Fagan, Brian (2003). *Before California: An archaeologist looks at our earliest inhabitants*. Lanham, MD: Rowman & Littlefield Publishers. ISBN 0742527948. OCLC 226025645 [2].
- Moratto, Michael J.; Fredrickson, David A. (1984). *California archaeology*. Orlando: Academic Press. ISBN 012506182X. OCLC 228668979 [3].

External links

- State of California [4]
- California travel guide from Wikitravel
- California [5] at the Open Directory Project
- 1973 documentary featuring aerial views of the California coastline from Mt. Shasta to Los Angeles [6]

Geographical coordinates: 37°N 120°W

krc:Калифорния frr:California pnb:کیلیفورنیا

Geography

Imperial Valley (California)

The **Imperial Valley** is a metropolitan and agricultural area of Southern California's Imperial County and northern region of Bajalta California. It is located in more southeastern Southern California, centered around the city of El Centro. Locally, the terms "Imperial Valley" and "Imperial County" are used synonymously. The Valley is bordered between the Colorado River to the east and, in part, the Salton Sea to the west. Farther west lies the San Diego and Imperial County border. To the north is the Inland Empire's Coachella Valley, which together form the "Cahuilla Basin" or the "Salton Trough", also the county line of Imperial and Riverside counties, and to the south the international boundary with the U.S. State of California and Baja California, Mexico.

The Imperial Valley is rich in natural beauty, local history, and culture. The unique culture of

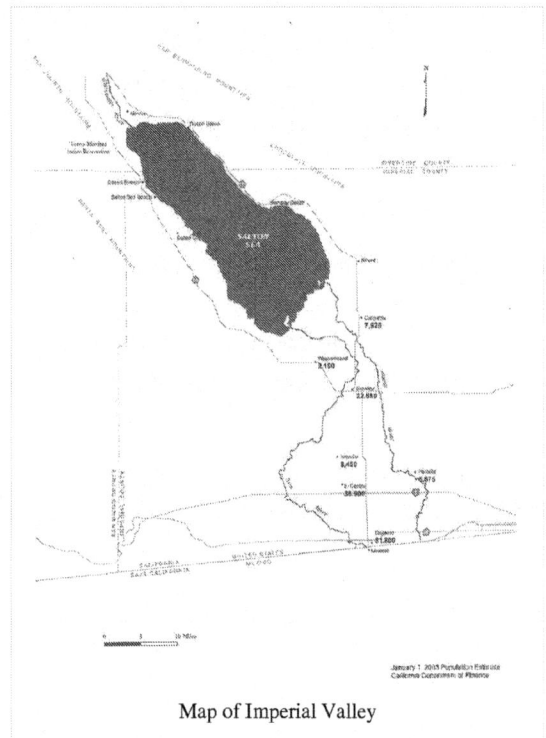

Map of Imperial Valley

the area blends the two different countries of the United States with Mexico, due to its regional history and geographic location along the international border. This creates a small town atmosphere, and an economy based on agriculture, and a strong work ethic for the people of the valley. From early in January through the winter holiday season, the Imperial Valley hosts many festivals and activities that keep things moving. From the aerial displays of the Blue Angels to the Tomato Festival. From the North to the South. Imperial Valley offers visitors and residents a taste of many cultures such as those from Mexico with all its' sights, sounds and tastes waiting to be savored. Mexico can easily be accessed by vehicle or by walking due to the Valleys proximity to the border.

Imperial Valley was so named by the Imperial Land Company, in hopes of attracting settlers. Having done that it is now the home of the El Centro metropolitan area and also an economic center of Californias', government defined, "South Border".

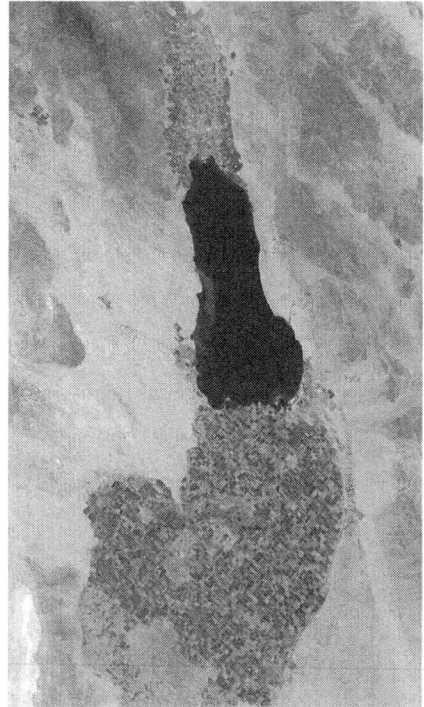

The Imperial Valley below the Salton Sea. The US-Mexican border is a diagonal in the lower left of the image.

Geography

The Valley is bordered between the Colorado River to the east and, in part, the Salton Sea to the west. Farther west lies the border with San Diego County, and to the south the international boundary with the U.S. State of California and Baja California, Mexico. To the north is the boundary with Inland Empire's Riverside County, and its Coachella Valley, which with the Imperial Valley form the "Cahuilla Basin" or the "Salton Trough".

The Imperial Valley extends southward for 50 miles (80 km) from the southern end of the Salton Sea into Mexico. Part of a trough stretching from the Coachella Valley to the Gulf of California, it is almost entirely below sea level—235 feet (72 m) below at the edge of the Salton Sea. Its hot desert climate is characterized by daily temperature extremes. It was once part of the Gulf of California, from which it was cut off by the dam-like deposits of the Colorado River Delta Fan as it carved out the Grand Canyon. Bordered by sand dunes and barren mountains, it was uninhabited until 1901, when the Imperial Canal was opened and diverted Colorado River water into the valley through Mexico. Floodwaters in 1905–07 destroyed the irrigation channels and created the Salton Sea now filled by the New River and irrigation run-off. The rivers in the southern part of the Salton Sea river basin flow south to north.

Bighorns in Anza-Borrego

Salton Sea

Climate

The Imperial Valley often has summer temperatures well over 100 degrees, however from late October until mid-April the temperature is relatively mild and can sometimes even reach low temperatures not expected in a desert. During winter months the Valley averages more than eight hours of sunshine a day, receiving the most sunlight of any place in the United States.[citation needed]

Historically, the lowest minimum temperature ever recorded in the Imperial Valley was 16 degrees F on January 22, 1937. The highest maximum temperature ever recorded was 121 degrees F on July 28, 1995. The lowest maximum temperature was 42 degrees F, recorded on January 24, 1949, and the highest minimum temperature was 92 degrees F on June 30, 1946. The highest monthly mean temperature was 95.9 degrees F, recorded in August 1969 and the lowest mean temperature was 42.3

degrees F in February 1939.

The 85-year average annual rainfall is 2.93 inches (74 mm) with June being the driest month. The only recorded snowfall in the Valley occurred on December 12, 1932. Snow began falling at 8:45 p.m. and by 5 a.m. The next day 2.5 inches (6 cm) had been recorded. In the southwest portion of Imperial Valley, 4 inches (10 cm) of snow was reported that day. This was the only snowfall of record to cover the entire valley.

Population

The El Centro Metropolitan Area is home to 163,972 residents, according to a 2008 US Census estimate and encompasses the whole Imperial County. The area is in the far southeast region of the State of California. Major population centers are Brawley, Calexico and El Centro which is the county seat. Imperial Valley is one of the fastest growing counties in the State of California offering many business opportunities along with a large number of trade possibilities.

Imperial County Courthouse in El Centro

Imperial County had the largest percentage increase in population in California between 2008 and 2009 in the state, according to the California Department of Finance. The county had a population growth rate of 2.2 percent between July 1, 2008, and July 1, 2009. The county's growth rate has consistently been one of the top 10 out of 58 counties in California for the past six years. Last year's growth rate was 2.43 percent.

El Centro is the promising new major commercial and industrial center of Southern California for the imperial valley, being the center of shipping exports as well as being home to retail, transportation, wholesale, and agricultural industries. There are also two international border crossings nearby for commercial and noncommercial vehicles. The city's population was 37,835 at the 2000 census. The 2006 population is 40,563. The city is 50 feet (20 m) below sea level and the largest city in the United States below sea level. Fifty percent of the jobs in El Centro come from the service and retail sector.

Regions

Imperial Valley can loosely categorize its cities and communities into three regions: the Salton Beach Towns, Desert Cities, and the El Centro area (urbanized Imperial). The Salton Sea Beach Towns have the smallest cities but were resorts in their heyday and have since shrunk in population and size due to the current state of the Salton Sea. The cities and communities of the desert region are outliers in that they are away from urbanized Imperial and tend to be smaller in population then the cities surrounding El Centro. Cities of the El Centro area tend to be larger than those of the desert and Salton regions.

Imperial Valley Cities

Cities over 10,000 population

- El Centro (County Seat)
- Calexico
- Brawley

Cities under 10,000 population

- Imperial
- Calipatria
- Holtville
- Westmorland

Towns over 1,000 population

- Heber
- Seeley
- Niland

Towns under 1,000 population

- Salton City
- Desert Shores
- Winterhaven

Salton City

- Salton Sea Beach
- Bombay Beach
- Ocotillo
- Palo Verde

Economics

Imperial County's economy consists predominantly of government, agriculture and retail trade that represents approximately 70% of total county employment. Government services account for over one-third of total employment. Agriculture accounts for one-fourth of jobs with major crops of alfalfa, lettuce, sugar beets and carrots. Retail growth has been experienced due to increased population in the Imperial and Mexicali Valleys. In 2005, the Imperial Valley Mall opened attracting shoppers from the Valley area, including residents and tourists across the border from Mexicali, greatly contributing to the county's retail sales.

Tourism

The secondary industry of the Imperial Valley: tourism. Many visitors come to the area to visit the Salton Sea (California's largest inland lake, which serves as a dumpout point for the overflow and drainage from the IID canal system and ditch drainage) and the Algodones Dunes. The New River and the Alamo River flow from the border city of Mexicali northward to the Salton Sea.

The Algodones Dunes

Another popular destination are the Salton Sea mud pots and volcanoes. These mud pots and volcanoes are located in an open field on the eastern side of the Salton Sea. The mud is just above ambient temperature and you can walk right up to the vents. However this is a natural system and temperatures will vary. Caution is advised. The location is host to a number of gray cones reaching heights of six feet (2 m) and depressions filled with bubbling mud. These features are the result of the geothermal activity in the area.

Off-roading on ATV's is also another popular activity for many Southern Californian's visiting the Imperial Valley. Many people from San Diego often take part in this activity during the summer months. Heber Dunes State Vehicular Recreation Area is located south of El Centro and is a primarily used off roading destination. The valley sand dune recreation area draws hundreds of thousands of off-road enthusiasts on good weekends. Outdoor enthusiasts will find plenty to do in the Imperial Valley. Another popular activity is bird watching do to natural habitats so abundant that bird watchers from around the globe come to glimpse rare species. The Imperial Valley combines water and sun to create a desert oasis that produces an array of excellent golf courses for all levels. Golf courses are in Holtville, Brawley and two in and around El Centro.

Sites of interest

Fort Yuma

Fort Yuma is located on the banks of the Colorado River in Winterhaven, California. First established after the end of the Mexican-American War in 1848, it was originally located in the bottoms near the Colorado River, less than 1 mile (2 km) below the mouth of the Gila River. It was to defend the newly settled community of Yuma, Arizona on the other side of the Colorado River and the nearby Mexican border. In March 1851 the post was moved to a small elevation on the Colorado's west bank, opposite the present city of Yuma, Arizona, on the site of the former Mission Puerto de Purísima Concepción. This site had been occupied by Camp Calhoun, named for John C. Calhoun, established in 1849. Fort Yuma was established to protect the southern emigrant travel route to California and to attempt control of the warlike Yuma Indians in the surrounding 100-mile (160 km) area.

Blue Angels

NAF El Centro is the winter home of the U.S. Navy Flight Demonstration Squadron, The Blue Angels. NAF El Centro historically kicks off the Blue Angels' season with their first air show, traditionally held in March.

Imperial Valley Expo & Fairgrounds

Home to the California Mid-Winter Fair and Fiesta which is the local county fair. It is also home to the Imperial Valley Speedway, a $\frac{3}{8}$ miles (600 m) race track.

Blue Angels

Algodones Sand Dunes

The name Algodones Dunes refers to the entire geographic feature, while the administrative designation for that portion managed by the Bureau of Land Management is the "Imperial Sand Dunes Recreation Area" (sometimes called the "Glamis Dunes"). The Algodones Sand Dunes are the largest mass of sand dunes in California. This dune system extends for more than 40 miles (60 km) along the eastern edge of the Imperial Valley agricultural region in a band averaging 5 miles (8 km) in width. A major east-west route of the Union Pacific railroad skirts the eastern edge.The dune system is divided into 3 areas. The northern most area is known as Mammoth Wash. South of Mammoth Wash is the North Algodones Dunes Wilderness established by the 1994 California Desert Protection Act. This area is closed to motorized use and access is by hiking and horseback. The largest and most heavily used area begins at Highway 78 and continues south just past Interstate 8. The expansive dune formations offer picturesque scenery,, a chance to view rare plants and animals, and a playground for ATV and off-roading enthusiasts. The dunes are also popular in film making and have been the site for movies such as Return of the Jedi.

Colorado River

The Colorado River is a popular destination for water sports including fishing, boating, water-skiing, and jet-skiing. The Colorado River is a river in the southwestern United States and northwestern Mexico, approximately 2,330 kilometres (1,450 mi) long, draining a part of the arid regions on the western slope of the Rocky Mountains. The natural course of the river flows from north of Grand Lake, Colorado into the Gulf of California. For many months out of the year, however, no water actually flows from the United States to the gulf, due to human consumption.

Salvation Mountain

Salvation Mountain (location 33°15'14.9"N 115°28'21.4"W) is a colorful artificial mountain north of Calipatria, California, near Slab City. It is made from adobe, straw, and thousands of gallons of paint. It was created by Leonard Knight to convey the message that "God Loves Everyone". Mr. Knight refused substantial donations of money and labor from supporters who wished to modify his message of universal love to favor or disfavor particular groups.

Anza-Borrego Desert State Park

Anza-Borrego Desert State Park, portions of which are located in Imperial County, is the largest state park in California. 500 miles (800 km) of dirt roads, 12 wilderness areas and miles of hiking trails provide visitors with an unparalleled opportunity to experience the wonders of the Colorado Desert. The park is named after Spanish explorer Juan Bautista de Anza and the Spanish name borrego, or bighorn sheep. The park features washes, wildflowers, palm groves, cacti and sweeping vistas. Visitors may also have the chance to see roadrunner, golden eagles, kit foxes, mule deer and bighorn sheep as well as iguanas, chuckwallas and the red diamond rattlesnake.

Fossil Canyon and Painted Gorge

Located near Ocotillo, California in the Coyote Mountains, Fossil Canyon and the surrounding area is a great place for rock hounding and fossil hunting. The fossils here are not dinosaurs, but ancient shells, coral, and oysters from the Miocene epoch when the area was underwater.

The Painted Gorge, located on the eastern side of the Coyote Mountains, consists of sedimentary, metamorphic and igneous rocks. Heat and movement over time has created fantastic shapes and colors. Oranges, reds, purples, and mauves mixed with browns and blacks create a palette of color as the sun illuminates and plays shadows upon this geologic wonder.

Imperial NWR

The Imperial National Wildlife Refuge protects wildlife habitat along 30 miles (50 km) of the lower Colorado River in Arizona and California, including the last un-channeled section before the river enters Mexico. The river and its associated backwater lakes and wetlands are a green oasis, contrasting with the surrounding desert mountains. It is a refuge and breeding area for migratory birds and local desert wildlife.

Sonny Bono Salton Sea NWR

The Sonny Bono Salton Sea National Wildlife Refuge is located 40 miles (60 km) north of the Mexican border at the southern end of the Salton Sea in California's Imperial Valley. Situated along the Pacific Flyway, the refuge is the only one of its kind, located 227 feet (69 m) below sea level. Because of its southern latitude, elevation and location in the Colorado Desert, the refuge experiences some of the highest temperatures in the nation. Daily temperatures from May to October generally exceed 100°F with temperatures of 116°-120°F recorded yearly.

Mexicali

The border city of Mexicali, Baja California, Mexico, offers big city amenities like museums, a zoo, a sports convention center, and an international airport. Visitors cross by foot or car from Calexico, California in the United States every day. Restaurants and taco stands, pharmacies, bars and dance clubs are part of the draw for the city's tourists. Many shops and stalls selling Mexican crafts and souvenirs are also located in walking distance from the border. Also many residents from California, Arizona and Nevada look for medical and dental services in Mexicali, because they tend to be less expensive than those in the United States. Mexico's drinking age of 18 (vs. 21 in the United States) makes it a common weekend destination for many high school and college aged Southern Californians. Thie town was near the epicenter of the 2010 Baja California earthquake.

Agriculture

Although this region is in the Colorado Desert section of the Sonoran Desert, with high temperatures and low average rainfall of 3 inches (75 mm) per year, the economy is heavily based on agriculture due to irrigation, which is supplied wholly from the Colorado River via the All-American Canal. Thousands of acres of prime farmland have transformed the desert into one of the most productive farming regions in California with an annual crop production of over $1 billion. Agriculture is the largest industry in the Imperial Valley and accounts for 48% of all employment. An environmental cost is that, south of the canal, the Colorado River no longer flows at all for much of the year.

The New River

A vast system of canals, check dams, and pipelines carry the water all over the valley, a system which forms the Imperial Irrigation District, or IID. The water distribution system includes over 1400 miles (2300 km) of canal and with 1100 miles (1800 km) of pipeline. The number of canal and pipeline branches number roughly over a hundred. Imported water and a long growing season allow two crop cycles each year, and the Imperial Valley is a major source of winter fruits and vegetables, cotton, and grain for U.S. and international markets. Alfalfa is another major crop produced in the Imperial Valley. The agricultural lands are served by a constructed agricultural drain system, which conveys surface runoff and subsurface drainage from fields to the Salton Sea, which is a designated repository for agricultural runoff, with environmental considerations not yet solved.

- All-American Canal
- All-American Canal Bridge
- Alamo Canal
- Coachella Canal
- Imperial Irrigation District
- Imperial Land Company
- California Development Company

Renewable Energy

Imperial Valley has become a "hot bed" of renewable energy projects, both solar and geothermal. This is driven in part by California's mandate to generate 20% of its power from renewable sources by the end of 2010, the valley's excellent sun resources, the high unemployment, its proximity to large population centers on the coast, and large tracts of otherwise unusable desert land.

Much of the land suitable for green energy is owned by the federal government (Bureau of Land

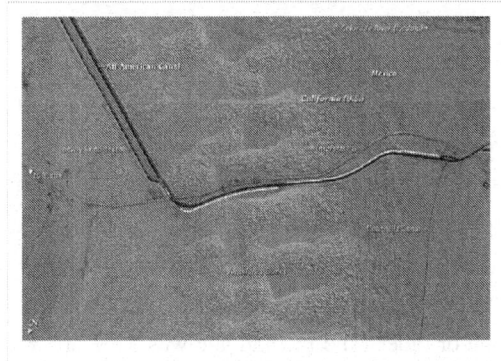

Management). As of April 2008, the BLM has received 163 applications to build renewable energy projects on 1600000 acres (6500 km^2) in California, "almost all of them are planned for the Imperial Valley and the desert region north of the valley." Stirling Energy is currently building one of the world's largest solar thermal plants, 10 square miles (26 km^2) with 38,000 "sun catchers," it will power up to 600,000 homes once it is fully operational by around 2015. CalEnergy currently runs a geothermal plant that generates 340 megawatts, enough power for 300,000 homes, and could tap into more for up to 2.5 million homes.

Demographics

The Imperial and Mexicali Valleys share a common international bond of both American and Hispanic cultures. On the U.S. side, the majority of residents are of Mexican-American or Latino heritage, while the Mexican side has been greatly influenced by American culture by the U.S. for many decades. The entire valley has multi-racial representation of Africans, Europeans, east and south Asians, and Native Americans.

As of the census of 2000, there were 142,361 people, 39,384 households, and 31,467 families residing in the county. The population density was 34 people per square mile (13/km²). There were 43,891 housing units at an average density of 10 per square mile (4/km²). The racial makeup of the county was 49.37% White, 3.95% Black or African American, 1.87% Native American, 1.99% Asian, 0.08% Pacific Islander, 39.08% from other races, and 3.65% from two or more races. 72.22% of the population were Hispanic or Latino of any race. 65.7% spoke Spanish and 32.3% English as their first language.

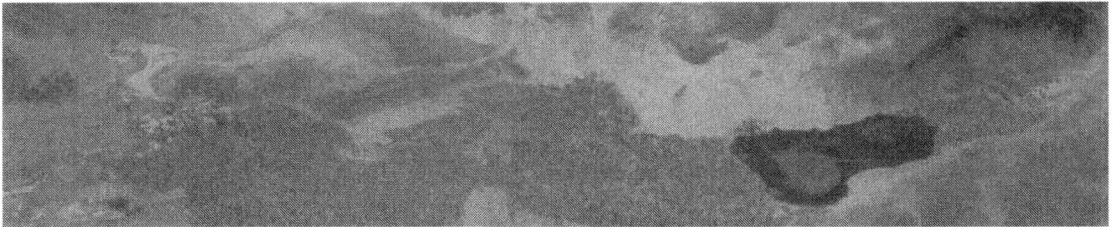

Laguna Salada, Mexicali Valley, Imperial Valley, Salton Sea, and Coachella Valley Left-Right

There were 39,384 households out of which 46.7% had children under the age of 18 living with them, 57.7% were married couples living together, 17.1% had a female householder with no husband present, and 20.1% were non-families. 17.1% of all households were made up of individuals and 8.1% had someone living alone who was 65 years of age or older. The average household size was 3.33 and the average family size was 3.77.In the county the population was spread out with 31.4% under the age of 18, 9.9% from 18 to 24, 30.4% from 25 to 44, 18.2% from 45 to 64, and 10.0% who were 65 years of age or older. The median age was 31 years. For every 100 females there were 109.3 males. For every 100 females age 18 and over, there were 111.4 males.

Presidential election results

Year	DEM	GOP	Others
2008	**61.1%** *17,761*	37.3% *10,850*	1.6% *459*
2004	**52.4%** *17,964*	46.4% *15,890*	1.2% *420*
2000	**53.5%** *15,489*	43.3% *12,524*	3.2% *924*
1996	**55.3%** *14,591*	36.8% *9,705*	8.0% *2,104*
1992	**43.9%** *11,109*	38.5% *9,759*	17.6% *4,450*
1988	43.8% *10,243*	**55.2%** *12,889*	1.0% *233*
1984	36.9% *8,237*	**62.0%** *13,829*	1.1% *235*
1980	36.9% *7,961*	**55.9%** *12,068*	7.2% *1,550*
1976	48.2% *10,244*	**49.9%** *10,618*	1.9% *400*
1972	34.9% *7,982*	**62.1%** *14,178*	3.0% *689*

Politics

Imperial County is a Democratic stronghold in Presidential, Congressional and local elections. The last Republican to win a majority in the county was George H. W. Bush in 1988.

On November 4, 2008, Imperial County voted 69.7% for Proposition 8, which amended the California Constitution to ban same-sex marriages, showing more support for the proposition than any other strongly Democratic county.

Imperial is part of California's 51st congressional district, which is held by Democrat Bob Filner. In the state legislature, Imperial is part of the 80th Assembly district, which is held by Democrat Manuel Perez, and the 40th Senate district, which is held by Democrat Denise Ducheny.

The median income for a household in the county was $31,870, and the median income for a family was $35,226. Males had a median income of $32,775 versus $23,974 for females. The per capita income for the county was $13,239. About 19.4% of families and 22.6% of the population were below the poverty line, including 28.7% of those under age 18 and 13.6% of those age 65 or over.

Education

Schools In The Imperial Valley

The Imperial Valley has many schools to offer education; high schools, middle/junior high school, elementary schools, and college. Central Union High School, Southwest High School and Brawley Union High School are some of the high schools Imperial Valley has to offer. Imperial Valley College, located in Imperial, California and SDSU Imperial Valley Extension, located in Calexico, CA are the colleges the Imperial Valley has to offer. The major high school rivals in the valley are the Central Union High School "Spartans" and Brawley Union High School "Wildcats"- these high school play an annual football game called the "Bell Game", whoever wins the game is victorious in the Imperial Valley League and keeps the bell. For two consecutive years (since 2008), the Spartans have kept the bell home. The bell game is held the second Friday of November. It is a game that almost everyone in the valley attends; the game gets very packed, the bleachers alway get full, and it gets full all around the football field.

Transportation

Major highways

- 🛡 Interstate 8
- ⑦ State Route 7
- ⑦⑧ State Route 78
- ⑧⑥ State Route 86
- ⑨⑧ State Route 98
- ⑪⑪ State Route 111
- ⑪⑤ State Route 115

Fish Creek Mtns

Public transportation

- Greyhound Lines
- Imperial Valley Transit
- Amtrak

Airports

Imperial County Airport is the main airport in the county. It is primarily a general aviation airport with limited commercial flight service. The major nearby airport is the San Diego International Airport.

Airport	IATA code	ICAO code	City
Calexico International Airport	CXL	KCXL	Calexico
Holtville Airport	L04	none	Holtville
Imperial County Airport	IPL	KIPL	Imperial

Culture

Due to its desert environment and proximity to Los Angeles, California, movies are sometimes filmed in the sand dunes outside the agricultural portions of the Imperial Valley. These have included

- *Return of the Jedi*
- *Independence Day*
- *Stargate*
- *The Scorpion King*
- *Into the Wild*

Additionally, portions of the 2005 film *Jarhead* were filmed here because of its similarity to the desert terrain of Iraq. Mountains that were visible in the background during filming were digitally removed during postproduction.[1]

See also

O. M. Wozencraft - "Father of the Imperial Valley"

External links

- City of El Centro Website [2]
- Imperial Valley Press Online [3]
- Imperial Valley's Online Video News [4]
- Imperial Valley Living [5]
- City of Imperial Website [6]
- Imperial Valley College [7]
- Imperial Valley Economic Development [8]
- Imperial Irrigation District [9]
- Concretions from Imperial Valley [10]

Geographical coordinates: 33°06′N 115°30′W

Colorado Desert

California's **Colorado Desert** is a part of the larger Sonoran Desert, which extends across southwest North America. The Colorado Desert region encompasses approximately 7 million acres (28000 km^2), reaching from the Mexican border in the south to the higher-elevation Mojave Desert in the north and from the Colorado River in the east to the Laguna Mountains of the Peninsular Ranges in the west. The area includes the heavily irrigated Coachella and Imperial Valleys. The Colorado Desert is home to many unique flora and fauna, many of which can be found no where else on the planet.

Geography and geology

The Colorado Desert region encompasses approximately 7 million acres (28000 km^2), reaching from the Mexican border in the south to the higher-elevation Mojave Desert in the north and from the Colorado River in the east to the Laguna Mountains of the Peninsular Ranges in the west. The desert encompasses Imperial County and includes parts of San Diego County, Riverside County, and a very small part of San Bernardino County.

The Algodones Dunes.

The majority of the Colorado Desert lies at a relatively low elevation, below 1000 feet (300 m), with the lowest point of the desert floor at 275 feet (84 m) below sea level at the Salton Sea. Although the highest peaks of the Peninsular Range reach elevations of nearly 10000 feet (3000 m), most of the region's mountains do not exceed 3000 feet (910 m).

In this region, the geology is dominated by the transition of the tectonic plate boundary from rift to fault. The southernmost strands of the San Andreas Fault connect to the northern-most extensions of the East Pacific Rise. Consequently, the region is subject to earthquakes, and the crust is being stretched, resulting in a sinking of the terrain over time.

Climate

The Colorado Desert's climate distinguishes it from other deserts. The region experiences greater summer daytime temperatures than higher-elevation deserts and almost never experiences frost. In addition, the Colorado Desert, especially toward the southern portion of the region, experiences two rainy seasons per year, in the winter and late summer, while the more northerly Mojave Desert has only winter rains.

The west coast Peninsular Ranges, or other west ranges, of Southern California–northern Baja California, block most eastern Pacific coastal air and rains, producing an arid climate. Other short, or longer-term weather events can move due north from the Gulf of California, including remnants of Pacific hurricanes, or storms from the southern tropical jetstream and the northern ITCZ, and are often active in the summer monsoons.

Flora and fauna

See also: List of plants by common name (Sonoran Desert)

See also categories: Fauna of the Sonoran Desert and Fauna of the Sonoran Desert

The region's terrestrial habitats include creosote bush scrub; mixed scrub, including yucca and cholla cactus; desert saltbush; sandy soil grasslands; and desert dunes. Higher elevations are dominated by pinyon pine and California juniper, with areas of manzanita and Coulter pine. In addition to hardy perennials, more than half of the desert's plant species are herbaceous annuals, and appropriately timed winter rains produce abundant early spring wildflowers. In the southern portion of the region, the additional moisture supplied by summer rainfall fosters the germination of summer annual plants and supports smoketree, ironwood, and palo verde trees. The unique Joshua Tree can be found in Joshua Tree National Park, as well as small regions of central or northwestern Arizona.

Bighorn Sheep at Palm Canyon in Anza-Borrego State Park.

Common desert wildlife include mule deer, bobcat, desert kangaroo rat, cactus mouse, black-tailed jackrabbit, Gambel's quail, and red-diamond rattlesnake. Among sensitive species are flat-tailed horned lizard, Coachella Valley fringe-toed lizard, desert tortoise, prairie falcon, Andrews' dune scarab beetle, Peninsular bighorn sheep, and California leaf-nosed bat.

In the Colorado Desert's arid environment, aquatic and wetland habitats are limited in extent but are critically important to wildlife. Runoff from seasonal rains and groundwater springs forms desert arroyos, desert fan palm oases, freshwater marshes, brine lakes, desert washes, ephemeral and perennial streams, and riparian vegetation communities dominated by cottonwood, willow, and non-native tamarisk. Two of the region's most significant aquatic systems are the Salton Sea and the Colorado River. While most desert wildlife depend on aquatic habitats as water sources, a number of species, such as arroyo toad, desert pupfish, Yuma clapper rail, and southwestern willow flycatcher, are restricted to these habitats. In some places, summer rains produce short-lived seasonal pools that host uncommon species like Couch's spadefoot toad.

Desert fan palm oases are rare ecological communities found only in the Colorado Desert. They occur only where permanent water sources are available, such as at springs or along fault lines, where groundwater is forced to the surface by the movement of hard impermeable rock, and can be found in the San Jacinto, Santa Rosa, and Little San Bernardino mountains, in the canyons of Anza-Borrego Desert State Park, and along the San Andreas Fault in the Coachella Valley. The only palm native to California, Washingtonia filifera (*Desert fan palm or California fan palm*), grow at the oases.

Endemic flora

Some sub-regions of the Colorado Desert contain endemic flora. Along the Lower Colorado River Valley, in-flow side canyons, flatlands, or low to higher level elevations, at least three endemic flora exist: *Hesperocallis undulata, Nolina bigelovii*, and *Peucephyllum schottii*, the Desert Lily, a Nolina bunchgrass, and the Desert fir.

National and State Parks

- Joshua Tree National Park
- Imperial NWR
- Sonny Bono Salton Sea NWR
- Indio Hills Palms
- Anza-Borrego Desert State Park
- Ocotillo Wells State Vehicular Recreation Area
- Picacho State Recreation Area
- Heber Dunes State Vehicular Recreation Area
- Salton Sea State Recreation Area

Environmental issues

Although the Colorado Desert remains one of the least-populous regions in California, human activities have had substantial impacts on the region's habitats and wildlife. Many unique communities, particularly aquatic and dune systems, are limited in distribution and separated by vast expanses of inhospitable, arid desert terrain. Even limited human disturbances can have markedly deleterious effects on the endemic and sensitive species supported by these unique regional systems.

Some of the greatest human-caused effects on the region have resulted from the water diversions and flood control measures along the Colorado River. These measures have dramatically altered the region's hydrology by redistributing the region's water supply to large expanses of irrigated agriculture and metropolitan coastal areas such as Los Angeles and San Diego. The once-dynamic Salton Sea and Colorado River ecosystems are now controlled by human water management. Because of the scarcity of water resources in the desert environment, these alterations have had substantial impacts on regional wildlife and habitats. In addition, portions of the region are experiencing substantial growth and development pressures, most notably the Coachella Valley.

See also

- Yuma Desert
- Sonoran Desert
- Mojave Desert
- Chihuahuan Desert
- List of North American deserts

External links

- Colorado Desert - Overview [1] from California Wildlife Action Plan [2] site

Colorado River

Geographical coordinates: 31°54′N 114°57′W

Colorado River	
'Aha Kwahwat, Seedskeedee, Río Colorado	
A remote stretch of the Colorado River from the Escalante Route in the Grand Canyon	
Countries	United States, Mexico
States	Colorado, Utah, Arizona, Nevada, California, Baja California, Sonora
Tributaries	
- left	Fraser River, Eagle River, Roaring Fork River, Gunnison River, Dolores River, San Juan River, Little Colorado River, Bill Williams River, Gila River
- right	Green River, Dirty Devil River, Escalante River, Kanab River, Virgin River, Hardy River
Source	La Poudre Pass Lake
- location	Rocky Mountain National Park, Colorado, United States
- elevation	10175 ft (3101 m)
- coordinates	40°28′20″N 105°49′34″W
Mouth	Gulf of California
- elevation	0 ft (0 m)
- coordinates	31°54′N 114°57′W
Length	1450 mi (2334 km)
Basin	246000 sq mi (637000 km²)

Discharge	for Lee's Ferry, 16 miles (26 km) below Glen Canyon Dam
- average	17850 cu ft/s (500 m^3/s)
- max	220000 cu ft/s (6200 m^3/s)
- min	700 cu ft/s (0 m^3/s)

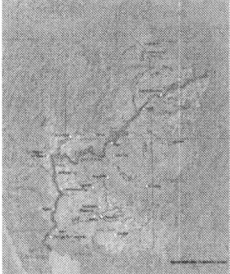

Map of the Colorado River watershed showing tributaries, lakes/reservoirs, cities and topography

The **Colorado River**, Mojave language **'Aha Kwahwat**, Spanish: ***Río Colorado (Red River)***, is a river in the Southwestern United States and northwestern Mexico, approximately 1450 miles (2330 km) long, draining a part of the arid regions on the western slope of the Rocky Mountains. The natural course of the river flows from the Continental Divide at La Poudre Pass in Rocky Mountain National Park, Colorado, into the Gulf of California between the Baja California peninsula and mainland Mexico. Large irrigation diversions for California's Imperial Valley through the All-American Canal, and to a much lesser extent irrigation diversions for Arizona, have dewatered the lower course of the river below Yuma, Arizona, resulting in it no longer consistently reaching the Gulf of California.

The watershed of the Colorado River covers 246000 sq mi (640000 km^2) in parts of seven U.S. states and two Mexican states.

Course

Headwaters

Near the source of the Colorado River in Rocky Mountain National Park, Colorado

The Colorado River's headwater is located in Rocky Mountain National Park about 25 mi (40 km). north of Lake Granby at the northern tip of Colorado's Grand County where Jackson County and Larimer County intersect. This is the unique geologic point where the Continental Divide intersects the Colorado River drainage basin to the west and the eastern flowing drainage basins for Jackson County's North Platte River and the Larimer County headwaters of the Laramie River, Cache La Poudre River and the northernmost main branch of the South Platte River. Below Rocky Mountain National Park, the river flows through the Kawuneeche Valley, also part of the Park, into Grand Lake, Colorado's largest and deepest natural lake. By law it can fluctuate no more than one vertical foot, so the Colorado River actually flows into Shadow Mountain Reservoir where it encounters the first of many dams in its journey to the Gulf of California. The physical connection between Shadow Mountain Reservoir and Grand Lake is not the course of the Colorado River, but a logistical piece of a larger trans-basin water storage and delivery project. This is the Colorado-Big Thompson Project that diverts the headwaters of the Colorado River to Colorado's Front Range and Eastern Plains on the other side of the Continental Divide. The next stop on the river's journey, Lake Granby, is used as a reservoir in this same project. Windy Gap Reservoir at the confluence of the Fraser and Colorado Rivers, west of the town of Granby, is another. From there, U.S. Highway 40 roughly parallels the river to the town of Kremmling, where the Blue River joins, before it enters Gore Canyon, to the west.

Many of the river's uppermost tributaries within Colorado are small. The rivers Fraser, Williams Fork and Blue enter below Granby and finally just below Kremmling, at the top of Upper Gore Canyon. There it drops significantly until 131 crosses at State Bridge. There are larger contributors, such as the Gunnison River and Roaring Fork River, in which massive amounts of water flow. About a hundred miles later it meets the Eagle River in the town of Dotsero, Colorado, and where I-70 parallels the river through Glenwood Canyon. The river then passes through the city of Glenwood Springs where it is joined by the swift flowing Roaring Fork River. West of Glenwood Springs, the Colorado runs through the Grand Valley and is joined by the Gunnison River at Grand Junction. From there it flows in an arc west-north to the Utah border and Westwater Canyon. Here, the Colorado ranges from 200 to 1200 ft (61 to 370 m) wide and from 6 to 30 ft (1.8 to 9.1 m) in depth with occasional deeper areas.

Canvas

Horseshoe Bend is a horseshoe-shaped meander of the Colorado River located near the town of Page, Arizona

The river turns southwest near Fruita, Colorado, and is joined by the Dolores River soon after entering Utah. It partially forms the southern border of Arches National Park near Moab, Utah, and then passes by Dead Horse Point State Park and through Canyonlands National Park where it is met by one of its primary tributaries, the Green River. The Colorado River then flows into Lake Powell, formed by the Glen Canyon Dam, where the San Juan River joins. Below the dam, water released from the bottom of Lake Powell makes the river clear, clean, and cold. Just south of the town of Page, Arizona, the river forms the dramatic Horseshoe Bend, then at Lees Ferry is joined by another tributary, the warm, shallow, muddy Paria River, and begins its course through Marble Canyon. Here, the Colorado River ranges from 175 to 700 ft (53 to 210 m) in width and 9 to 130 ft (2.7 to 40 m) in depth.

At the southern end of Marble Canyon, the river is joined by another tributary, the Little Colorado River, and the river then turns abruptly west directly across the folds and fault line of the plateau, through Grand Canyon and Grand Canyon National Park, which is 349 km long (217 miles) and from 6 to 30 km (4 to 20 miles) between the upper cliffs. The walls, 4000 to 6000 ft (1200 to 1800 m) high, drop in successive escarpments of 500 to 1600 ft (150 to 490 m), banded in splendid colors toward the narrow gorge of the present river.

Below the confluence of the Virgin River in Nevada, the Colorado River abruptly turns southward. Hoover Dam, built during the Great Depression, forms Lake Mead, a popular recreation site as well as the supplier of most of the water for the Las Vegas metropolitan area. From Hoover Dam, the river flows south and forms part of the boundary between Arizona and Nevada and between Arizona and California. Along the California-Arizona reach of the river, four additional dams are operated to divert water for municipal supplies and agricultural irrigation, and for recreational uses. Lake Mohave, formed by Davis Dam, lies in the southern portion of the Lake Mead National Recreation Area. Lake Havasu, formed by Parker Dam, provides recreation as well as the home of the retired U.K. London Bridge, now the New London Bridge. The two remaining dams supply irrigation water: Palo Verde Diversion Dam and Imperial Dam. Here, the Colorado River ranges in width from 700 to 2500 ft (210 to 760 m) and from 8 to 100 ft (2.4 to 30 m) in depth.

Final course

Below the Black Canyon the river lessens in gradient and in its lower course flows through the Colorado Desert in a broad sedimentary valley's distinct estuarine plain upriver from Yuma, where it is joined by the Gila River. The channel through much of this region is bedded in a dike-like embankment lying above the floodplain over which the escaping water spills in time of flood. This dike cuts off the flow of the river to the remarkable low area in southern California known as the Salton Sink in the Coachella Valley, and the Imperial Valley. The Salton Sink and its Salton Sea are located below sea level; therefore, the descent from the river near Yuma is very much greater than the descent from Yuma to the Gulf of California.

The lower course of the river—which forms the border between the Mexican state of Sonora on the mainland and the state of Baja California on the Baja California peninsula—is a dry or small stream most of the year due to the river being diverted into the Imperial Valley's irrigation source, the All-American Canal. Several miles from its mouth, the Hardy River enters, adding a little water to the often dry Colorado before it reaches the Gulf of California.

Prior to the mid 20th century, the Colorado River Delta provided a rich estuarine marshland; while today it is now essentially desiccated, the river is still an important ecological estuary resource. The estuary of the Colorado River was subjected to a major tidal bore that has almost disappeared with the drastic reduction in the freshwater flow following the irrigation diversions of the Colorado River, and to a lesser extent because of some dredging of the estuary channel. The first historical record of the tidal bore was that of the Croatian missionary in Spanish service Father Ferdinand Konščak on 18 July 1746. During spring tide conditions, the tidal bore formed in the estuary about Montague Island and propagated upstream. It was called locally 'El Burro' or 'burro'. Today the tidal bore is rarely seen although there are still some anecdotal observations.

Discharge

The Colorado River's discharge has been modified by large dams and diversions for irrigation, resulting in a reduction of the river's discharge along its lower course. The diversions are principally responsible for reducing the average flow of the Colorado near its mouth from about 22000 cubic feet per second (623 m^3/s) between 1903 and 1934 to less than 4000 cubic feet per second (113 m^3/s) from 1951 to 1980. Annual flow near the river's mouth in 1984 was 17500 cubic feet per second (496 m^3/s) due to record-breaking precipitation. From 1975 to 2004 the average flow at the US–Mexico border was 2661 cubic feet per second (75 m^3/s).

The United States Geological Survey (USGS) operates a number of stream gauges along the Colorado River. A gauge on its middle course, at Lee's Ferry, 16 miles (26 km) below Glen Canyon Dam, recorded an average discharge of 17850 cubic feet per second (505 m^3/s) between 1895 and 2009. The maximum flow recorded at this station was 220000 cubic feet per second (6230 m^3/s) on June 18, 1921. The minimum flow was 700 cubic feet per second (20 m^3/s), January 23–24, 1963, resulting from the construction of Glen Canyon Dam. The mean annual discharge recorded by downriver gauges are all lower than at the Lee's Ferry gauge, and includes 13860 cubic feet per second (392 m³/s) below Hoover Dam, 14190 cubic feet per second (402 m³/s) below Davis Dam, 12040 cubic feet per second (341 m³/s) below Parker Dam, 1724 cubic feet per second (49 m³/s) below the Laguna Diversion Dam, and 1988 cubic feet per second (56 m³/s), for 2008–2009, at the Northerly International Boundary (NIB) with Mexico, 1.1 miles (1.8 km) above Morelos Dam. This NIB gauge has operated since 1950 and is, via the International Boundary and Water Commission, the accounting point for the 1944 International Treaty detailing water delivery to Mexico.

The last stream gauge is at the Southerly International Boundary (SIB), where the river leaves the United States altogether. Although the river flows about 75 miles (121 km) from the SIB to its mouth, no discharge data has been collected since 1983. The amount of water that reaches the mouth of the Colorado River is not known. It is often estimated to be similar to that recorded at the SIB even though this is probably inaccurate. Accounts of flow below the SIB range from zero to a level equal to that recorded at the SIB. The average annual discharge at the SIB from 1975 to 2004 was 1,928,000 acre-feet per year, or 2661 cubic feet per second (75 m³/s). During that period's 18 "non-surplus" years the flow at the SIB was only 865,000 acre-feet per year, or 1194 cubic feet per second (34 m³/s). There has been no measurable flow at all at the SIB for extended periods during many years. In 1996 no flow was recorded on any day of the entire year. Nonetheless, a small amount of water flows into the Colorado River below the SIB, mostly from irrigation returns, the Hardy River, and effluent from the cities of San Luis Río Colorado and Mexicali.

History

First inhabitants

Several groups of ancient nomadic people, descended from Uto-Aztecan speakers, sparsely populated the Colorado Plateau thousands of years ago. In about 6,000 B.C., the Hisatsinom, predecessor of the Puebloan peoples, emerged near the Four Corners region around the San Juan River, while about 500 B.C., people of the Fremont culture began to populate the area around the Green River and the eastern part of the Great Basin. It was not until about 700 A.D. that the ancestral Puebloans began to cultivate crops for food, and the famous cliff dwellings for which they are best known did not come into being until past 1000 A.D.

Native American groups such as the Anasazi, Navajo, Pueblo and Hohokam Indians later lived on the arid lands of the Colorado Plateau, using water from the Colorado and its tributaries for irrigation. These two native groups formed large agriculture-based societies which each only lasted for a few hundred years, starting from around 200 B.C. The Anasazi inhabited the northern part of the Plateau and the foothills of the Rockies, in areas such as Chaco Canyon near the San Juan and Green Rivers, while the Hohokam lived in present-day central Arizona in the Gila River valley around the confluence with the Salt River. Both the Anasazi and Hohokam utilized extensive systems of canals to water their farmland, with over 220 miles (350 km) utilized by the Hohokam alone.

Native civilization reached its peak from 600 to 900 A.D. in the Colorado watershed, but began a general decline afterwards. Around the 13th century and 14th century, near the height of a second peak, the Anasazi and Hohokam cultures suddenly "disappeared" from the lands around the Colorado River. Their demise is believed to be linked to the overuse of water for irrigation combined with a severe half-century drought. Intensive irrigation raised the water table while increasing the salinity of the soils used for farming, eventually making them unsuitable. Flash floods during the 12th century and 13th century were probably responsible for the demise of the Chaco culture, and the Navajo and Puebloan people who lived in the high desert in the Four Corners region near present-day Lake Powell declined as well.

It is believed that during the severe droughts of the three centuries surrounding the 13th century, many of the peoples that once inhabited the upper regions of the Colorado watershed migrated to the Rio Grande valley and the Painted Desert in the Little Colorado River region. Many of the people in the Hopi and Zuni tribes of the Sonoran Desert, as well as the Acoma and Laguna people on the Rio Grande, are believed to be descended from the ancient inhabitants of the northeastern Colorado Plateau.

Downstream view of the Colorado River at river mile 175 in the Grand Canyon

Early records

The existence of the Colorado River was first noted in the records of written history in September, 1539, when Francisco de Ulloa sailed to the head of the Gulf of California and rowed a short distance upstream. It was next seen by Hernando de Alarcon who in 1540 led the maritime contingent of Coronado's expedition. The plan was to meet the land based force and resupply them. Alarcon ascended the river about 85 miles to the limit of navigation near present-day Yuma, Arizona. He waited for Coronado, but eventually despaired, cached some supplies and correspondence, left a note on a tree, and departed. Coronado's land forces never reached that location, but Melchior Diaz, on his third expedition, went to see if he could establish contact with Alarcon. By the time he reached the Colorado, however, Alarcon had already left. The Native Americans told him what they knew of Alarcon's presence and that he had left a cache of supplies. Diaz found the note and the supplies. Diaz named the river *Rio del Tizon* ("River of Embers" or "Firebrand River") based on a practice used by the natives for warming themselves. Meanwhile, Coronado (who at the time was near Zuni, New Mexico) had learned from one of his scouting parties that the natives spoke of a large river to the west. He sent Garcia Lopez de

Cardenas to lead a contingent of men to find this river. They did find it at what is now known as the Grand Canyon, becoming the first people of European background to see it. Their failed attempts at reaching the river led them to conclude that it would not be possible to be supplied via the Gulf of California and the river.

The following year, Francisco de Bolanos sailed to the mouth of the river on the Gulf of California. One of his pilots, Domingo del Castillo, prepared a map of the Mexican coast. He charted three rivers at the head of the gulf and named them *Brazo de laguna p.*, *Rio de buena Guia p.*, and *Brazo de Mira flores p.*. The latter of these three is the longest. Later references suggest that *Brazo de Mira flores* referred to what is now called the Gila River, and that *Rio de buena Guia* was his name for the Colorado. In spite of these records, the legend and mapmaking error showing an Island of California

Colorado River in the Grand Canyon from Desert View

persisted for more than a century, especially among European cartographers.

Comparisons of 17th, 18th, and early 19th-century maps reveal a parade of names being applied to the Colorado and its tributaries, as well as a variety of courses, as cartographers learned or made up the geography of the region. On a map by Nicholas Sanson (1650) the *R. del Tecon* and the *R. de Coral* share a common mouth on the gulf. A number of maps show the Gila River (sometimes just the lower, sometimes the whole) as the *Rio Grande de las Apostoles*. A 1763 map by Emanuel Bowen equates the Apostles with the *del Coral*. A 1720 map by Fer Nicholas labels the main body of the Colorado as Rio del Tison, and a tributary of the Apostles/Gila as Rio Colorade. In 1703 Guillaume de L'Isle showed a *Rio de buena esperanza* as a major tributary of the *Tison*, but it is not clear if this tributary corresponds better with the Little Colorado or the San Juan. A map by Herman Moll (1720) charts the *Tison* and the Gila with separate mouths. Upriver from a tributary of the *Tison* that would appear to correspond with today's Virgin River, the name for the main channel is given as R. of Good Hope. On other maps Good Hope/*Buena Esperanza* are transferred to a tributary of the Gila. A map of 1757 gives the name of the main course as *Rio Colorado de los Martyres*. A map of 1781 by Jonathan Carver charts a major split in the river and labels the eastern branch "Colorado" and the western branch *Martyres*. A map from 1758 by Didier Robert de Vaugondy applies the name Colorado to a river that reaches north to the headwaters of the Missouri, best corresponding to today's Green River. When Jedediah Smith first reached the lower Colorado in 1826, he first called it the Seedskeedee, as the headwaters of the Green River were known to the trappers, but also noted that the natives called it the Colorado.

The Colorado River from Laughlin

It is not clear when or why the name "Colorado" first replaced "Tizon" (Tecon/Tison), which had been the most common name on maps since 1540. Among the maps in the Library of Congress, every use of "Colorado" (or Colorade) from 1720 and before is applied to a tributary of what is now the Gila River that seems best to correspond with today's Verde River. The earliest map in that collection that replaces "Tizon" with "Colorado" is a map from 1743.

The map that resulted from Escalante's expedition in 1776 labels the main channel as the Colorado up to the confluence of the Nabajoo and Zaguananas rivers. The associated information leads one to conclude that the Nabajoo corresponds to the San Juan and the Zaguananas to the Colorado from there to the Dolores River. On this map the Colorado above the Dolores is called the Rafael, and the Green River (named Buenaventura River) is erroneously diverted to the southwest and to what is now called Sevier Lake. Where Escalante's journal records his crossing of the San Rafael, he notes that the Native Americans knew this river as the Colorado. He also notes that the natives said this river had it source in a distant lake, but the lake is not charted on the resulting map. It is evident from a number of maps of the period that people were not aware of the distance between the Colorado's confluence with the Dolores and the western slopes of the Front Range. On a map from 1847 by John Disturnell, the Rafael is replaced with the Green River, while the upper Colorado (or more correctly, what would be called the Grand River) is not shown at all.

Grand River

"Grand River" is the name applied to the Colorado River from its headwaters in Rocky Mountain National Park to its confluence with the Green River in Utah from about 1836 to 1921. This gave rise to several now orphaned names including Grand Lake, Grand Valley, Grand Junction, Grand County, Colorado, and Grand County, Utah. The earliest appearance of this name on a map could be on the map by Henry Schenck Tanner (1836). The name there replaces the name of Rio Rafael, which appears on many earlier maps. The head of this branch of the Colorado is shown as at about the same latitude as Longs Peak in Colorado. There is nothing charted that corresponds to the Green River, nothing that corresponds with the course of the Dolores (even though some earlier maps did show the Dolores with reasonable accuracy), and the headwaters of both the Rio Grande ("Rio del Norte") and especially the Arkansas River are shown to reach to a higher latitude.

A map by David H. Burr (1839) shows the "Colorado River of the West" flowing from the headwaters of the Green River to the Gulf of California, with the "Grand River" as a tributary branching to the east, the third tributary upriver from the Nabajoo (San Juan). The Green River is not separately named. The headwaters of the Grand are depicted as being very close to the headwaters of the Rio Grande (which is labeled "Rio Bravo del Norte") as well as those of the Arkansas River. A textual note on the map indicates that little is known of this area. In 1859, a U.S. Army topographic expedition led by Captain John Macomb located the confluence of the Green River with the Grand River in what is now Canyonlands National Park. The Macomb party designated the confluence as the source of the Colorado River.

In 1921, U.S. Representative Edward T. Taylor petitioned the Congressional Committee on Interstate and Foreign Commerce to rename the Grand River as the Colorado River. On July 25, 1921 the name change was made official in House Joint Resolution 460 of the 66th Congress, over the objections of representatives from Wyoming and Utah and the United States Geological Survey which noted that the drainage basin of the Green River was more than 70% more extensive than that of the Grand River, although the Grand carried a slightly higher volume of water at its confluence with the Green.

Elevation summary

Approximate heights above sea level at several key locations:

Feet	Meters	Location
9000	2750	Colorado headwaters (Rocky Mountains)
6100	1850	midway to Colorado-Utah border
4300	1300	Colorado-Utah border
3850	1170	midway to Utah-Arizona border
3700	1130	Utah-Arizona border (Wahweap Bay)
3000	900	midway to Grand Canyon (Rider Point)
2800	850	Grand Canyon North Rim
2500	760	Grand Canyon South Rim
1200	365	Lake Mead (above Hoover Dam)
600	183	below Hoover Dam
485	150	California-Nevada-Arizona border
100	30	California-Arizona-Mexico border

Note that the significant difference between the present height of the rim of the Grand Canyon (about 2440 m; 8000 ft) and the levels at which the river enters/exits it gives rise to the geologic theory that its upheaval must have begun around the same time the river began flowing through it and eroding it (since rivers do not run uphill, it would have otherwise followed some other path around the upheaval). Estimates for the beginning of this erosion/upheaval process range from 5 to 70 million years ago.

Engineering

Main article: Salton Sea

In California in the autumn of 1904, the river's waters escaped into a diversion canal a few miles below Yuma, Arizona, creating the New River and Alamo River, and over two years re-forming the Salton Sea in the Salton Sink of the Coachella Valley. The river re-created the Salton Sea, a great inland sea in the Salton Sink, an area that it had frequently inundated before. For example, in 1884 and 1891 the river practically abandoned its regular course through Mexico to the Gulf of

Glen Canyon Dam and Lake Powell

California, and flowed into the Salton Sink. However, it was effectively dammed in the early part of 1907 and it returned to its normal course, although from which there was still much leakage to the Salton Sea. In July 1907 the permanent dam was completed, keeping the Colorado's usually normal course from the Black Canyon through the Colorado Desert basin towards the Gulf of California.

From the Hoover Dam

The Colorado River is a major and in some cases life-sustaining source of water for irrigation, drinking, and other uses by people living in the arid American southwest. Allocation of the river's water is governed by the Colorado River Compact. Several dams have been built along the Colorado River, beginning with Glen Canyon Dam near the Utah-Arizona border. Other dams include Hoover Dam, Parker Dam, Davis Dam, Palo Verde Diversion Dam, and Imperial Dam. Since the completion of the dams, the majority of the river in normal hydrologic years is diverted for agricultural and municipal water supply. The Colorado's last drops evaporate in the Sonoran Desert, miles before the river reaches the Gulf of California. Almost 90% of all water diverted from the river is for irrigation purposes. The All-American Canal is the largest irrigation canal in the world and carries a volume of water from 420 to 850 m³/s (15,000 to 30,000 ft³/s), making it larger in volume than New York's Hudson River. The canal's waters are used to irrigate the fertile Imperial Valley orchards and crops, formerly a Sonoran Desert ecosystem where several years can pass between measurable rainfalls. Hydrology transport models are used to assess management of the river's flow and water quality.

Hoover Dam (originally *Boulder Dam*, and the first dam of its type) was completed in 1936. Its impoundment of the river in the Mojave Desert creates Lake Mead, which provides water for irrigation and the generation of hydroelectric power.

Several cities such as Phoenix and Tucson (Central Arizona Project-CAP), Los Angeles and San Bernardino (Colorado River aqueduct), Las Vegas, Nevada, and San Diego, California have aqueducts leading all the way back to the Colorado River. The Central Arizona Project (CAP) canal, which was begun in the 1970s and finished in the 1990s, begins at Parker Dam and runs all the way to Phoenix and then Tucson to supplement those cities' water needs.

The lower Colorado is navigable by moderate to large-sized craft. The lower river from Davis Dam to Yuma is navigable by large paddlewheel boats and river barges, but commercial navigation on the river is unimportant because the river is cut off from the sea, making other means of transportation more efficient in the region. Before the railroads arrived, the lower Colorado River from the sea to near present-day Laughlin, Nevada was an important means of transportation via large steamers. Most of the rest of the river (and reservoirs), excluding the rapids in the canyons, is navigable by small to moderate-sized river craft and power boats.

Glen Canyon Dam and Bridge

Moab uranium tailings

Main article: Moab Tailings

Atlas Mineral Corporation operated a uranium processing mill in the area of Moab, Utah, on the north bank of the Colorado River just under 5 km (about 3 miles) from downtown Moab. As a byproduct of uranium processing activities, an estimated 16 million ton pile of chemically and radioactively hazardous tailings exists. The pile is located about 700–800 feet from the Colorado River. Although no contamination has been detected, the proximity of the material to the watershed has been a concern. The Senate has authorized the U.S. Department of Energy to budget $22.8 million in 2007 to begin the project of moving the uranium tailings farther from the river. The plan is to move the contaminated materials 30 miles (48 km) north to a disposal site located at Crescent Junction, Utah. The project is expected to be completed by 2028 with current funding plans, at total estimated cost of US$720 million.

Fish species

The Colorado River basin is home to fourteen native species of fish. Four are endemic and endangered: Colorado pikeminnow (formerly Colorado squawfish), razorback sucker, bonytail chub, and humpback chub. The Upper Colorado River Endangered Fish Recovery Program is a controversial [citation needed] effort by the US Fish and Wildlife Service, in conjunction with the Arizona Game and Fish Department, the Colorado Division of Wildlife, and the Utah Department of Wildlife to recover these endangered fish.

Fish species in the river are Brook Trout, Catfish (Channel), Carp, Crappie, Largemouth Bass, Rainbow Trout, Striped Bass, Sunfish, Sturgeon, Colorado Pikeminnow, Humpback Chub, Razorback Sucker, Bonytail Chub, Smallmouth bass and Flathead Catfish

The Colorado River in James M. Robb - Colorado River State Park as the morning sun rises

See also

- Alamo Canal
- All-American Canal Bridge
- Colorado River Compact
- Colorado River Delta
- Colorado River Irrigation Company
- Salton Sea
- Glen Canyon Dam; Lake Powell
- Hoover Dam; Lake Mead
- Parker Dam; Lake Havasu
- List of tributaries of the Colorado River
- List of Colorado River rapids and features
- List of flora of the Lower Colorado River Valley
- Powell Geographic Expedition of 1869

Notes and references

Notes

References

@ This article incorporates text from a publication now in the public domain: Chisholm, Hugh, ed (1911). *Encyclopædia Britannica* (Eleventh ed.). Cambridge University Press.

External links

- Federal Department of Energy site on uranium mine tailing site. [1]
- State of Utah site on uranium mine tailings. [2]
- Bibliography on Water Resources and International Law [3] Peace Palace Library
- Arizona Boating Locations Facilities Map [4]
- Arizona Fishing Locations Map [5]
- Where to Fish in Arizona Species Information [6]
- Drought Watch Campaign [7] - map of the Colorado River system showing the fill levels of major reservoirs. Last updated July 2004.

Chocolate Mountains

Geographical coordinates: 33°27′57.100″N 115°35′0.958″W

Chocolate Mountains	
Mountain Range	
Country	United States
State	California
District	Imperial County
Coordinates	33°27′57.100″N 115°35′0.958″W
Highest point	
- elevation	877 m (2877 ft)
Timezone	Pacific (UTC-8)
- summer (DST)	PDT (UTC-7)
Topo map	USGS Frink NE

Main location of Chocolate Mountains in California
(a southeast portion abuts the Colorado River)

The **Chocolate Mountains** of California are located in Imperial County and Riverside County in the Colorado Desert in Southern California. The mountains stretch more than 60 miles (100 km) in a northwest to southeast direction, and are located east of the Salton Sea and south and west of the Chuckwalla Mountains and the Colorado River. To the northwest lie the Orocopia Mountains.

Geography

The mountains are located about 30 miles west of the Chocolate Mountains of Arizona, but the two ranges are not connected. The range reaches an elevation of 2,475 feet (754 m) at Mount Barrow.

The mountains receive very little rainfall in a normal year, typically 4-6 inches (100 to 150 mm). The predominant natural plants are of the creosote bush–white bursage community, and the mean annual temperature is about 60 °F to 75 °F (16 °C to 24 °C).

History

The Bradshaw Trail passed by the side of the mountains, the first "euroamerican" route to the Colorado River from Riverside, California

Military closures

The mountain range is occupied by the Chocolate Mountain Aerial Gunnery Range, an aerial and gunnery practice area used by the US Navy and Marines. A large part of the Chocolate Mountains lie within the gunnery range, and are off-limits to the public.

Areas near the mountains can be dangerous—in one instance, two jet pilots practicing dropping empty bombs overshot the gunnery range and bombed a public campground north of the mountains, injuring one man.

Geology

The Chocolate Mountains contain the world's richest gold rift zone. "Geologists estimate that the gold contained in this zone is worth between $40 to $100 billion. These are surface gold deposits which are more profitable to mine than the one-mile deep gold deposits in South Africa."[citation needed] When the gunnery range closes in the future, and the mountains are cleared of dangerous materials remaining from bombing practice, mining will most likely begin. The gold area was owned by the Catellus Development Corporation, now part of the industrial property giant ProLogis.

Wilderness Areas

Little Picacho Wilderness

The southeastern end of the Chocolate Mountains range is home to two important wilderness areas The first is the Little Picacho Wilderness, a 38,170 acre (154.5 km²) region of geological features and habitat protection under the direction of the Bureau of Land Management. The preserve has within its boundaries the southern portion of the Chocolate Mountains. Elevations within this area range from 200 to 1,500 feet. The topography, characterized by jutting spires and steep ridges, is quite dramatic. Ravines laced within the range gradually broaden into sandy, tree-lined washes. Slopes and plains are devoid of vegetation, instead covered with a desert pavement of angular cobbles. These rusty dark orange and brown colored cobbles stand out against the nearly white bottoms of the washes. It is also called the Little Picacho Peak Wilderness [1].

Indian Pass Wilderness

The Indian Pass Wilderness Area [2] is to the north with 32,008 acres of open space. The Indian Pass Wilderness is a distinctive part of the Chocolate Mountains, a range which extends from south central Riverside County to the Colorado River near Yuma, Arizona. Quartz peak is the highest point in the wilderness capped at 2,200 feet. Jagged peaks and spires are sliced by mazes of twisting canyons which carry water from occasional desert cloudbursts into several tree-lined washes. One of these washes passes through the heart of the wilderness area, giving rise to the region's local name, "Julian Wash country." The area's proximity to the Colorado River and the Arizona Desert contribute to the presence of wildlife species not commonly found in the California Desert.

At the southern end of the Chocolate Mountains at elevations from 200 to 1,500 feet, the Indian Pass Wilderness preserve is located 50 miles west of Brawley, California, and is also managed by the Bureau of Land Management. A herd of 25 Desert Bighorn Sheep are also reside in the wilderness area, and also "the Picacho Feral horses," wild burros, and the native and endangered Desert Tortoise and Spotted bat.

External links

- Official **Little Picacho Peak Wilderness website** [1]
  - BLM Little Picacho Peak Wilderness Map [3]
  - Little Picacho Peak Wilderness Area photographs [4]
- Official **Indian Pass Wilderness website** [2]
  - BLM Indian Pass Wilderness Map [5]

See also

- Category: Mountain ranges of the Colorado Desert
- Category: Protected areas of the Colorado Desert
- Category: Wilderness Areas within the Lower Colorado River Valley
- Category: Flora of the California desert regions

Cities/Towns in Imperial County

El Centro, California

City of El Centro

— City —

Imperial County Courthouse in El Centro

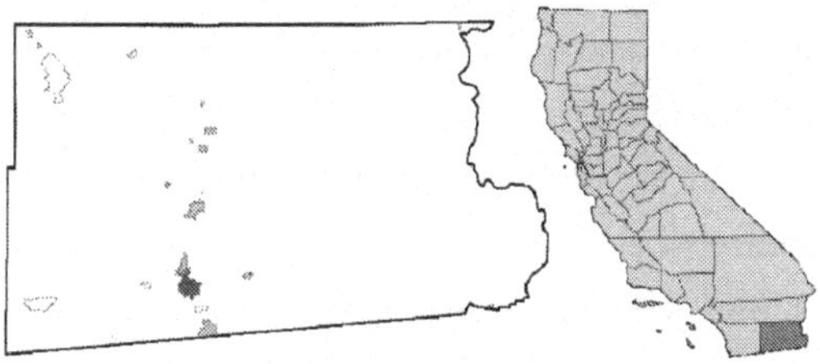

Location in Imperial County and the state of California

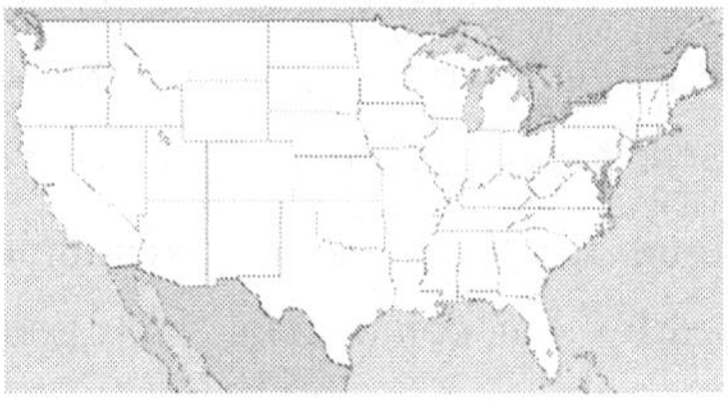

City of El Centro

Location in the United States

Coordinates: 32°47′31″N 115°33′47″W

Country	United States

State	California
Incorporated	April 16, 1908
Area	
- Total	9.6 sq mi (24.9 km^2)
- Land	9.6 sq mi (24.8 km^2)
- Water	0 sq mi (0.1 km^2)
Elevation	-39 ft (-12 m)
Population (2006)	
- Total	40563
- Density	3941.1/sq mi (1519.5/km^2)
Time zone	Pacific (PST) (UTC-8)
- Summer (DST)	PDT (UTC-7)
ZIP codes	92243-92244
Area code(s)	760
FIPS code	06-21782
GNIS feature ID	1656501

El Centro is the core urban area and principal city of the El Centro metropolitan area which encompasses all of Imperial County. The city is the county seat of Imperial County, the largest city in the Imperial Valley and the east anchor of the Southern California Border Region. El Centro is also the largest American city to lie entirely below sea level (- 50 feet). The city is conveniently near the global cities of San Diego and Los Angeles as well as placed between the major cities of Phoenix and San Diego.

Founded in 1906 W. F. Holt and C.A. Barker purchased the land on which El Centro was eventually built for about forty dollars an acre and invested $100,000 in improvements. As one historian of Valley life put it, *"in only five months El Centro went from a barley field to a city..."*.

It is home to retail, transportation, wholesale, and agricultural industries. There are also two international border crossings nearby for commercial and noncommercial vehicles. The city's population was 37,835 at the 2000 census. The 2006 population is 40,563. As of June 2010, El Centro has the highest unemployment rate among American cities, at 27.6%.

Geography

El Centro is located at 32°47′31″N 115°33′47″W.

According to the United States Census Bureau, the city has a total area of 9.6 square miles, (24.9 km²), of which 9.6 square miles, (24.8 km²), of it is land and 0.04 square miles, (0.1 km²), of it is water.

El Centro is located in the Imperial Valley(considered locally as synonymous with Imperial County). The city is 50 feet below sea level and the largest city in the United States below sea level. The Imperial Valley is in the Colorado Desert, an extension of the larger Sonoran Desert.

The agriculture industry's demand for water is supplied by canals diverting water from the nearby Colorado River. The Salton Sea was created after a 1905 flood from the Colorado River.

In this region, the geology is dominated by the transition of the tectonic plate boundary from rift to fault. The southernmost strands of the San Andreas Fault connect the northern-most extensions of the East Pacific Rise. Consequently, the region is subject to earthquakes, and the crust is being stretched, resulting in a sinking of the terrain over time.

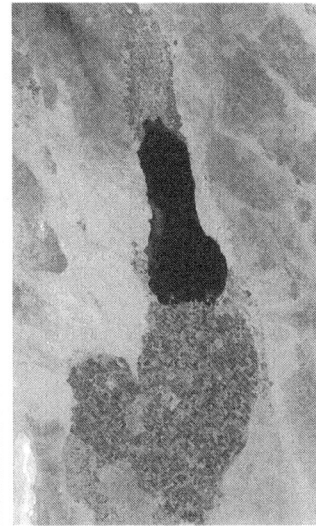

The Imperial Valley, as seen from the Space Shuttle. North is to the upper right. The Salton Sea is at the center. The US-Mexican border is a diagonal in the lower left.

History

Juan Bautista de Anza Bezerra Nieto

Spanish explorer Melchior Díaz was one of the first Europeans to visit the area around El Centro and Imperial Valley in 1540. The explorer Juan Bautista de Anza also explored the area in 1776 (an elementary school in El Centro now bears his name). Years later, after the Mexican-American War, the northern half of the valley was annexed by the U.S., while the southern half remained under Mexican rule. Small scale settlement in natural acquifer areas occurred in the early 19th century (the present-day site of Mexicali), but most permanent settlement (Anglo Americans in the U.S. side, Mexicans in the other side) was after 1900.[citation needed]

Originally part of San Diego County, the Imperial Valley was settled by farmers once water from the Colorado River was diverted via canals to irrigate the desert valley floor.[citation needed]

In 1906, the land on which El Centro was later built was purchased by W. F. Holt and C.A. Barker.

By 1907 Imperial County was incorporated into California and by then much of the valley was successfully irrigated.[citation needed]

Before the town began, the railroad had established a station and named the place Cabarker. The name honored C.A. Barker, a friend of the landowner. The first post office in El Centro opened in 1905.

The City of El Centro was incorporated on April 16, 1908. By 1910, the population of the city had reached 1,610. By 1920 it was 5,646. One reason for this rapid growth was El Centro's becoming the county seat of Imperial Valley.

Population growth was slow, but accelerated in the 1930s, again in the World War II era (1940s) despite the city was hard hit by a 7.1 earthquake in July 1940. [citation needed]

By the mid-1940s, El Centro had become the second largest city in the Imperial Valley, with a population of about 11,000 people. El Centro had also become the location of the Imperial Irrigation District (IID) administrative offices.

Agriculture has been an important industry within El Centro since the 1940s, because of its strategic location near rail lines and Highway 80 and 99 – more than 35 growers and shippers still operate in El Centro. However, by the early 1980s the two largest employment sectors in El Centro were Government and Wholesale/Retail Trade, reflecting El Centro's emerging role as a regional administrative and commercial center.

Sites of interest

Main article: Imperial Valley

The nearby Algodones Dunes, the largest dune field in the US, draws thousands of visitors each year, mainly for off-road driving. The Salton Sea lies 30 miles north of El Centro, but water sport enthusiasts head to the Colorado River, 50 miles to the east near Yuma, Arizona. The El Centro Naval Air Station 10 miles to the west is home to the annual Blue Angels flight maneuvering event. Stark Field is home of a minor league baseball team El Centro Imperials of the Arizona Summer League. Mexico (the border city of Mexicali, Baja California) is 10 miles away, which offers big city amenities like museums, a zoo and a sports convention center.

Climate

El Centro has an arid climate and is the southern-most desert city in the US with an elevation below sea-level. El Centro has over 350 days of sunshine and under 3 inches (76 mm) of rain annually. Winter temperatures are in the mid 70s to mid 80s with over-night lows in the low 50s to mid 40s. During summer days, the dry, desert heat can push temperatures well into the 100s, while the nights stay in the low 80s to mid 70s. Average annual humidity is 24%.[citation needed] Snow is almost totally unknown in the town, except for a very brief falling of sleet mixed with hail during a shower in December 1967.

Climate data for El Centro, California													
Month	Jan	Feb	Mar	Apr	May	Jun	Jul	Aug	Sep	Oct	Nov	Dec	Year
Record high °F (°C)	90 (32.2)	93 (33.9)	101 (38.3)	109 (42.8)	116 (46.7)	121 (49.4)	122 (50)	121 (49.4)	120 (48.9)	112 (44.4)	98 (36.7)	95 (35)	122 (50)
Average high °F (°C)	70 (21.1)	75 (23.9)	79 (26.1)	86 (30)	94 (34.4)	103 (39.4)	107 (41.7)	106 (41.1)	101 (38.3)	91 (32.8)	78 (25.6)	70 (21.1)	88 (31.1)
Average low °F (°C)	41 (5)	45 (7.2)	49 (9.4)	54 (12.2)	61 (16.1)	68 (20)	76 (24.4)	77 (25)	71 (21.7)	59 (15)	47 (8.3)	41 (5)	57 (13.9)
Record low °F (°C)	18 (-7.8)	24 (-4.4)	29 (-1.7)	34 (1.1)	36 (2.2)	47 (8.3)	52 (11.1)	54 (12.2)	48 (8.9)	33 (0.6)	24 (-4.4)	22 (-5.6)	18 (-7.8)
Precipitation inches (mm)	0.51 (13)	0.36 (9.1)	0.31 (7.9)	0.05 (1.3)	0.03 (0.8)	0.01 (0.3)	0.06 (1.5)	0.32 (8.1)	0.36 (9.1)	0.35 (8.9)	0.17 (4.3)	0.43 (10.9)	2.96 (75.2)
Source:													

Economy

As of 2009 the employment of El Centro residents is dominated by the local government, California state government, and federal government. Two nearby prisons and the U.S. Border Patrol provide employment; *The Economist* states that the prisons and border patrol were "relatively untouched" by the late-2000s recession. The El Centro area has many farming plots, where carrots, lettuce, and other crops are produced, and therefore the El Centro economy is subject to seasonal variations like other farming areas. Between November and March in winter periods, El Centro-area farmers harvest lettuce for $8–10 per hour. During March the harvest moves to the north and is no longer in El Centro; in previous eras farmers migrated, while in the first decade of the 21st century many collect unemployment benefits during the summer.

El Centro is surrounded by thousands of acres of farmland that has transformed the desert into one of the most productive farming regions in California with an annual crop production of over $1 billion. Agriculture is the largest industry in Imperial County and accounts for 48% of all employment.

Being the commercial center of Imperial County, fifty percent of the jobs in the El Centro come from the service and retail sector.

A recent growth in the interest of Imperial County as a filming location, has spurred growth in servicing this industry. Due to its desert environment and proximity to Los Angeles, California, movies are sometimes filmed in the sand dunes outside the agricultural portions of the Imperial County. These have included *Return of the Jedi*, *Stargate*, *The Scorpion King*, and *Into the Wild*. Additionally, portions of the 2005 film *Jarhead* were filmed here because of its similarity to the desert terrain of

Iraq.[citation needed]

El Centro during the late-2000s recession

According to the Bureau of Labor Statistics, as of April 30, 2009 the El Centro area had a 25.0% unemployment rate, the highest for a Metropolitan Area in the country. By August of that year, El Centro's unemployment rate was 27.5%, three times the overall United States unemployment rate of 9.7%. *The Economist* stated that the city is not the "centre of the Great Recession" like the figure would appear to indicate. While El Centro has a seasonal farming economy, there is still a fixed "baseline" unemployment at 12%. Timothy Kelly, the head of the Imperial Valley Economic Development Corporation, estimated that between 40,000 to 60,000 residents of Mexicali work in El Centro. *The Economist* added that there are likely many El Centro residents who work in Mexicali and collect unemployment benefits in El Centro; Ruben Duran, the city manager of El Centro, said that if the Mexicali jobs were factored into the employment rate, El Centro would have a normal employment rate. Francisca German, the manager of a job search agency called One Stop, said that about 3,000 people per month come into her agency; she says that some make a genuine effort to find jobs, while many do not have motivation to actually find a job, but to instead show proof that they tried to find a job. Kelly stated that unemployment fraud does not account for all of the issues with the El Centro area; he said that many residents have a lack of education and a lack of English language proficiency, so some of them cannot find jobs. *The Economist* added that the collapse of the housing market eliminated some construction jobs; the magazine countered that the scenario is true in many places in the United States. In December 2008 listed as #5 on Forbes.com's list of "The Top 10 Places in America Where Homes are Losing their Value Fastest" with 31.4% of homeowners owing more on their mortgages than their homes are worth. A national report on the effects of the "Great recession" of 2008/09 has found El Centro and the Imperial Valley in the top 5 poorest medium-sized cities in the U.S. in poverty and unemployment rates.

Culture

While the majority of the residents in this community are Hispanic, there is a diverse population with a wide array of interests. In the winter residents race on nearby sand dunes using four wheel drive buggies. During the summer residents spend time indoors instead of outside. Spanish is a dominant language among residents and over the radio. Many area residents live in both the United States and Mexico and go across the border frequently.

Demographics

As of the census of 2000, there were 37,835 people, 11,439 households, and 8,910 families residing in the city. The population density was 3,950.2 people per square mile (1,524.9/km²). There were 12,263 housing units at an average density of 1,280.3/sq mi (494.2/km²). The racial makeup of the city was 46.86% White, 3.16% Black or African American, 0.98% Native American, 3.50% Asian, 0.10% Pacific Islander, 41.68% from other races, and 3.73% from two or more races. 74.58% of the population were Hispanic or Latino of any race.

There were 11,439 households out of which 47.4% had children under the age of 18 living with them, 53.9% were married couples living together, 18.7% had a female householder with no husband present, and 22.1% were non-families. 18.8% of all households were made up of individuals and 7.3% had someone living alone who was 65 years of age or older. The average household size was 3.23 and the average family size was 3.71.

In the city the population was spread out with 33.6% under the age of 18, 9.7% from 18 to 24, 28.9% from 25 to 44, 18.5% from 45 to 64, and 9.3% who were 65 years of age or older. The median age was 30 years. For every 100 females there were 96.6 males. For every 100 females age 18 and over, there were 93.5 males.

The median income for a household in the city was $33,161, and the median income for a family was $36,910. Males had a median income of $36,753 versus $24,514 for females. The per capita income for the city was $13,874. About 20.6% of families and 22.8% of the population were below the poverty line, including 29.5% of those under age 18 and 14.8% of those age 65 or over.

In 2009 the Latinos in El Centro mainly consisted of dual citizens and permanent resident card (green card) holders. Illegal immigrants tended to go through Imperial County instead of staying in Imperial County.

Education

Within its boundary, there are three school districts – McCabe Union Elementary School District, El Centro School District and The Central Union High School District.

El Centro has 11 Elementary schools, 3 Middle/Junior High schools and 3 High Schools:

Elementary Schools

- St. Mary's Catholic School
- De Anza Magnet School
- Desert Garden Elementary School
- Harding Elementary School
- McCabe Elementary School
- McKinley Elementary School

- Margaret Hedrick Elementary School (named after a woman who had been teaching and working in schools for 55 years, 35 of them in the El Centro School system).
- Martin Luther King Jr Elementary School
- Meadows Elementary School
- Lincoln Elementary School
- Sunflower Elementary
- Washington Elementary School

Middle and Junior High Schools

- Corfman Middle School (Grades 4–8)
- Kennedy Middle School
- Woodrow Wilson Junior High

High Schools

The Central Union High School District includes two four-year comprehensive high schools(Central Union and Southwest) and one alternative education school(Desert Oasis). The school district's 3,450 students are supported by more than 350 certified and classified staff. The District is governed by a five member Board of Trustees.

- Central Union High School (Central Union was established near the time when the city was established and celebrated its 100th year in 2008.)
- Desert Oasis High School
- Southwest High School

Colleges and universities

Opportunities to attend college are available through Imperial Valley College, a local 2-year college, and an extension of San Diego State University located in Calexico, CA. San Diego State University's Calexico Campus offers a variety of Bachelors and Masters degrees.

Transportation

Freeways and highways

There are three major highways that serve El Centro. Interstate 8 connects San Diego to the west and Yuma, Arizona to the east. California State Route 86 and California State Route 111 parallel each other as they go north to Brawley before running along the west and east shores of the Salton Sea, respectively, on their way to the Palm Springs area. Going south from El Centro, Highway 86 terminates at Highway 111 before the latter runs to Calexico and Mexicali, Mexico

Public transportation

Imperial Valley Transit is the primary provider of mass transportation in the Imperial Valley. Formed in 1989 with just 3 buses and serving just 3000 people per month, the agency now currently serves more than 45,000 riders within the area per month.

Airports

Imperial County Airport is located in nearby Imperial. Service is subsidized by the Essential Air Service program. The nearest large international airports are San Diego International Airport and Mexicali International Airport.

Politics

El Centro is operated by a council/manager form of government. The members of the City Council also sit as the Community Development Commission (Commission) and Redevelopment Agency (Agency) governing boards. The City Manager is empowered as the Executive Director of the Commission and Agency.

In the state legislature El Centro is located in the 40th Senate District, represented by Democrat Denise Moreno Ducheny, and in the 80th Assembly District, represented by Democrat Manuel Perez. Federally, El Centro is located in California's 51st congressional district, which has a Cook PVI of D +7 and is represented by Democrat Bob Filner.

External links

- City of El Centro website [1]
- El Centro Chamber of Commerce and Visitors Bureau [2]
- El Centro Earthquake 1940 [3]
- El Centro travel guide from Wikitravel

Calexico, California

City of Calexico	
— City —	
Location of Calexico, California	
Coordinates: 32°40′44″N 115°29′56″W	
Country	United States
State	California
County	Imperial
Government	
- Mayor	Louis Fuentes
Area	
- Total	6.2 sq mi (20.38 km^2)
- Land	6.2 sq mi (20.38 km^2)
- Water	0.0 sq mi (0 km^2)
Elevation	7 ft (2 m)
Population (2009)	
- Total	39,000(approx.)
- Density	4351.4/sq mi (1680.1/km^2)
Time zone	PST (UTC-8)
- Summer (DST)	PDT (UTC-7)
ZIP codes	92231-92232
Area code(s)	760
FIPS code	06-09710
GNIS feature ID	1652680

Website	http://www.calexico.ca. gov

Calexico is a city in Imperial County, California. The population was 27,109 at the 2000 census. Calexico is about 122 miles (196 km) east of San Diego and 62 miles (100 km) west of Yuma, Arizona. The name "Calexico" is a portmanteau of California "Cal~" and Mexico "~exico", which like that of the adjacent city of Mexicali, emphasizes its importance as a border city.

More than 60,000 people pass through Calexico per day. The Police Department of Calexico consists of about 8 patrol cars on duty at any one time. However, their traffic department has about 25 employees that patrol and control traffic and intersections often clogged by border commuters.[citation needed]

Major events every year are the Mariachi festival on March 25 followed by the SDSU "Perspective of the Latino Race" art exhibition on April 3.

Curtis Hanson's *Losin' It* was filmed in Calexico.

The band Calexico is named after the town.

Geography

Calexico is located at 32°40′44″N 115°29′56″W.

According to the United States Census Bureau, the city has a total area of 6.2 square miles (16.1 km²), all of it land. Calexico is located 230 miles (370 km) southeast of Los Angeles, 125 miles (201 km) east of San Diego, 260 miles (420 km) west of Phoenix, Arizona, and adjacent to Mexicali, Baja California, Mexico.

Calexico's location provides easy overnight trucking access to all those transportation hubs plus the ports of Long Beach, California, and Ensenada, Baja California, Mexico.

Calexico's strategic location is seen by many as the prime link between the interior of Mexico and the major markets along the west coast of the U.S. and Canada.

Calexico is served by State Routes 98, 7 and 111, with direct connection to Interstate 8 (5 miles north) and State Route 86. There are eighteen regular and irregular common carriers for intrastate and interstate truck service to Calexico.

Rail service is provided by Union Pacific Railroad, and connects with the main line to Portland, Oregon; Rock Island, Illinois; Tucumcari, New Mexico; St. Louis, Missouri; and New Orleans, Louisiana.

Within city limits is Calexico International Airport, the U.S. Customs and Border Protection check-point for private passenger and air-cargo flights entering the U.S. from Mexico. Private charter services are also available there.

General aviation facilities and scheduled passenger and air-cargo service to Los Angeles International Airport, Phoenix Sky Harbor International Airport, and other points are available at Imperial County Airport (Boley Field), located 17 miles (27 km) north.

History

Calexico began as a tent city of the Imperial Land Company and has grown into a large, thriving city on the U.S.-Mexico border. Calexico was founded in 1899 and incorporated in 1908. The Imperial Land Company converted bone-dry desert land into a fertile setting for year-round agriculture that provides an economic base. The originally proposed names were *Santo Tomas* or *Thomasville*.

The first settlers were Mexicans, since Calexico lies on the Mexican border. After the Mexican Revolution of the 1910s, thousands of Mexican refugees settled in the Imperial Valley on the U.S. side. Today, Calexico is said to hold the highest percentage of Latino residents of any city in the U.S. (about 90%).[citation needed] However, only 49% are of Mexican descent and 35% are born in Mexico, followed by those born in Central America totals at 16%. [citation needed]

Although it gained a reputation for a while as a typical U.S.-Mexico bordertown with all the tawdry aspects usually associated with such places, the modern city of Calexico is a far cry from what it was back in those early days. Hundreds of acres are now being devoted to industrial parks, and commercial and retail incentives are being offered to encourage industrial development.

Since Calexico represents the mixing of two cultures and areas and because of its proximity to the Mexican border, the name Calexico was coined from a combination of the words California and Mexico. Mexicali is a similarly-named city directly across the international border from Calexico.

The first post office in Calexico opened in 1902.

2010 Earthquake

Main article: 2010 Baja California earthquake

On April 4, 2010 the city was struck by a 7.2 magnitude earthquake centered just across the Mexican border. A state of emergency was declared and First and Second streets between Paulin and Heber Avenues was cordoned off. Two buildings partially collapsed downtown and a large amount glass and debris littered the streets. The Calexico water treatment plant sustained severe damage.

Government

The City of Calexico operates under a City Council/City Manager form of government. The City Council consists of five Council Members, elected to overlapping four-year term. The Mayor and Mayor Pro-Tem are chosen from among the five council members and rotate on an annual basis.

The Mayor presides at council meetings, where all official policies and laws of the City are enacted. The members of the Calexico City Council set policy and appoint commissions and committees that study the present and future needs of Calexico.

The other two elected officials in the City of Calexico are the City Clerk and City Treasurer. Each of them is elected directly by the voters and serves a four year term.

The Calexico branch of the Imperial County Superior Court system was officially renamed on Saturday, December 19, 1992 in honor of Legaspi family members Henry, Victor and Luis Legaspi as the Legaspi Municipal Court Complex.

Demographics

As of the census of 2000, there were 27,109 people, 6,814 households, and 5,982 families residing in the city. The population density was 4,353.4 people per square mile (1,680.1/km²). There were 6,983 housing units at an average density of 1,121.4/sq mi (432.8/km²).

The racial makeup of the city was 46.56 percent White, 0.49 percent Black or African American, 0.67 percent Native American, 1.81 percent Asian, 0.02 percent Pacific Islander, 46.99 percent from other races, and 3.45 percent from two or more races. With 95.29 percent of the population Hispanic or Latino (of any race), Calexico has one of the highest Hispanic/Latino percentages of any California city.

There were 6,814 households out of which 53.4 percent had children under the age of 18 living with them, 61.2 percent were married couples living together, 22.0 percent had a female householder with no husband present, and 12.2 percent were non-families. 10.4 percent of all households were made up of individuals and 6.9 percent had someone living alone who was 65 years of age or older. The average household size was 3.96 and the average family size was 4.21.

In the city the population was spread out with 34.9 percent under the age of 18, 9.9 percent from 18 to 24, 27.1 percent from 25 to 44, 17.6 percent from 45 to 64, and 10.4 percent who were 65 years of age or older. The median age was 29 years. For every 100 females there were 87.2 males. For every 100 females age 18 and over, there were 80.6 males. The rate of teen pregnancy in the city is ranked third in the nation with 17.3 percent of females between the ages of 14 and 18 being pregnant.

The median income for a household in the city was $28,929, and the median income for a family was $30,277. Males had a median income of $27,712 versus $18,857 for females. The per capita income for the city was $9,981. About 22.6 percent of families and 25.7 percent of the population were below the poverty line, including 30.8 percent of those under age 18 and 16.2 percent of those age 65 or over. The poverty rate in Calexico as a border city is above-average in the US, while in contrast Mexicali is considered prosperous by Mexican standards.

Politics

In the state legislature Calexico is located in the 40th Senate District, represented by Democrat Denise Moreno Ducheny, and in the 80th Assembly District, represented by Democrat Manuel Perez. Federally, Calexico is located in California's 51st congressional district, which has a Cook PVI of D +7 and is represented by Democrat Bob Filner.

Education

Colleges and universities

Post-secondary education is available at the San Diego State University Imperial Valley Campus of San Diego State University, and at Imperial Valley College. In addition, there are more than 20 local agencies and programs providing vocational training which can be tailored to the specific needs of potential employers.

Public schools

The Calexico Unified School District serves city residents.

Elementary

[K-6] Kennedy Gardens Elementary-Home of the Eagles

Allen and Helen Mains Elementary-Home of the Trojans

Rockwood Elementary-Home of the Rockets

Blanche Charles Elementary-Home of the Dolphins

Jefferson Elementary-Home Of the Tigers

Dool Elementary-Home of the Cougars

Cesar Chavez Elementary-Home of the Lobos

Junior high schools

[7-12]

Willam Moreno Jr. High-Home of the Aztecs

Enrique Camarena Junior High School-Home of the Firebirds

[9]

De Anza Jr. High-Home of the Bullpups

Secondary schools

[10-12]

Calexico High School- Home of the Bulldogs

Aurora High School-Home of the Eagles

Adult education schools

Robert F. Morales Adult Education Center

Independent Studies Office

Private schools

Calexico Mission School, a Seventh-day Adventist Academy operated by the Southeastern California Conference [1] in Riverside, CA provides private religious education in Calexico from K-12.

Our Lady of Guadalupe Academy (Home to the Bees), and Vincent Memorial Catholic High School (Home to the Scott's), Roman Catholic schools operated by the Roman Catholic Diocese of San Diego, are also in Calexico.

Notable people

- Anita Álvarez de Williams - anthropologist and photographer
- Dan Navarro - singer/songwriter
- Enrique Castillo - actor
- Enrique Camarena -DEA Agent
- Tino Cuéllar - President Obama's Advisor on Immigration policy; an attorney and professor of law at Stanford University.
- Emilio Delgado - actor
- Bob Huff - California senator
- Takashi Kijima - photographer
- Ruben Niebla - baseball player
- Allen Strange - composer

- Eugenio Elorduy Walther - Governor of Baja California
- Bob Wilson - US Congressman

See also

- San Diego–Imperial, California
- El Centro Metropolitan Area

External links

- City of Calexico website [2]
- Calexico Chamber of Commerce [3]
- Calexico Unified School District [4]
- Camarena Memorial Library website [5]

Brawley, California

City of Brawley	
— City —	
Location in Imperial County and the state of California	
Coordinates: 32°58′43″N 115°31′49″W	
Country	United States
State	California
County	Imperial
Area	
- Total	5.8 sq mi (15.1 km^2)
- Land	5.8 sq mi (15.1 km^2)
- Water	0 sq mi (0 km^2)
Elevation	-112 ft (-34 m)
Population (2000)	
- Total	22052
- Density	3802.1/sq mi (1460.4/km^2)
Time zone	Pacific (PST) (UTC-8)
- Summer (DST)	PDT (UTC-7)
ZIP code	92227
Area code(s)	760
FIPS code	06-08058
GNIS feature ID	1656443

Brawley (formerly, **Braly**) is a city in Imperial County, California, United States. Brawley is located 13 miles (21 km) north of El Centro. The population was 22,052 at the 2000 census. The town has a significant cattle and feed industry, and hosts the annual Cattle Call Rodeo. Year-round agriculture is an important economic activity in Brawley. Summer daytime temperatures often exceed 120 °F (49 °C).

History

The Imperial Land Company laid out the town in 1902 and named it Braly in honor of J.H. Braly, who owned the land. After Braly refused to permit the use of his name, the name was changed to Brawley. The first post office at Brawley opened in 1903.

Incorporated in 1908, it was a "tent city" of only 100 persons involved in railroads and the earliest introduction of agriculture. It had a population of 11,922 in 1950, but population growth was slow from the 1960s to the early 1990s.

Geography

Brawley is located at 32°58′43″N 115°31′49″W.

According to the United States Census Bureau, the city has a total area of 5.8 square miles (15.1 km²), all land except for the Alamo and New Rivers that pass through the town (the latter of which has been reported as the most polluted river in North America). Brawley's elevation (like other Imperial Valley towns) is below sea level.

Climate

Average January temperatures in Brawley are a high of 69.4 °F (20.8 °C) and a low of 38.9 °F (3.8 °C). Average July temperatures are a high of 107.6 °F (42.0 °C) and a low of 75.2 °F (24.0 °C). There are an average of 177.0 days with highs of 90 °F (32 °C) or higher. There an average of 11.3 days with lows of 11.3 °F (−11 °C) or lower. The record high temperature was 122 °F (50 °C) on July 1, 1950, and the record low temperature was 4 °F (−16 °C) on January 1, 1919.

Average annual precipitation is 2.65 inches (6.7 cm). There an average of 13 days with measurable precipitation. The wettest year was 1939 with 8.18 inches (20.8 cm). There have been years when no measurable precipitation fell in Brawley, including 1953. The most rainfall in one month was 6.75 inches (17.1 cm) in September 1939. The most rainfall in 24 hours was 3.90 inches (9.9 cm) on October 10, 1932. A rare snowfall in December 1932 brought a total of 3.0 inches (7.6 cm).

Demographics

As of the census of 2000, there were 22,052 people, 6,631 households, and 5,265 families residing in the city. The population density was 3,783.0 people per square mile (1,460.4/km²). There were 7,038 housing units at an average density of 1,207.4/sq mi (466.1/km²). The racial makeup of the city was 52.78% White, 2.45% Black or African American, 1.11% Native American, 1.31% Asian, 0.19% Pacific Islander, 37.86% from other races, and 4.32% from two or more races. 73.83% of the population were Hispanic or Latino of any race.

There were 6,631 households out of which 48.0% had children under the age of 18 living with them, 56.0% were married couples living together, 17.5% had a female householder with no husband present, and 20.6% were non-families. 17.1% of all households were made up of individuals and 7.1% had someone living alone who was 65 years of age or older. The average household size was 3.28 and the average family size was 3.71.

In the city the population was spread out with 34.5% under the age of 18, 9.6% from 18 to 24, 28.2% from 25 to 44, 18.1% from 45 to 64, and 9.6% who were 65 years of age or older. The median age was 30 years. For every 100 females there were 96.9 males. For every 100 females age 18 and over, there were 92.5 males.

The median income for a household in the city was $31,277, and the median income for a family was $35,514. Males had a median income of $34,617 versus $25,064 for females. The per capita income for the city was $12,881. About 22.5% of families and 26.6% of the population were below the poverty line, including 34.0% of those under age 18 and 14.1% of those age 65 or over.

The majority of Brawley's residents today are of Mexican and Latino origins; the town contained white, East Indian, Chinese, Filipino and African American sections in the 20th century.

Politics

In the state legislature Brawley is located in the 40th Senate District, represented by Democrat Denise Moreno Ducheny, and in the 80th Assembly District, represented by Democrat Manuel Perez. Federally, Brawley is located in California's 51st congressional district, which has a Cook PVI of D +7 and is represented by Democrat Bob Filner.

Education

- High-school age students in both Brawley and neighboring Westmorland use the Brawley Union High School District, while children from kindergarten through eighth grade use the Brawley Elementary School District.
- San Diego State University operates a satellite campus in Brawley.

Public safety

Brawley maintains its own police and fire departments.

Notable people

- Sid Monge was a pitcher in Major League Baseball for the San Diego Padres, Philadelphia Phillies, Detroit Tigers, Cleveland Indians and California Angels.
- Sergio Romo is a relief pitcher in Major League Baseball for the San Francisco Giants.
- Rudy Seánez is a relief pitcher in Major League Baseball for the Philadelphia Phillies.
- Dr. Barbara O'Brien is the Lieutenant Governor of Colorado.
- Steve Taylor is a contemporary Christian singer, songwriter, record producer and film director.

See also

- El Centro Metropolitan Area
- San Diego–Imperial, California

External links

- City of Brawley website [1]
- Brawley Chamber of Commerce [2]

Imperial, California

City of Imperial	
— City —	
Location in Imperial County and the state of California	
Coordinates: 32°50′51″N 115°34′10″W	
Country	United States
State	California
County	Imperial
Area	
- Total	3.9 sq mi (10.1 km^2)
- Land	3.9 sq mi (10.1 km^2)
- Water	0 sq mi (0 km^2)
Elevation	-59 ft (-18 m)
Population (2006)	
- Total	11,754
- Density	1938.5/sq mi (748.5/km^2)
Time zone	Pacific (PST) (UTC-8)
- Summer (DST)	PDT (UTC-7)
ZIP code	92251
Area code(s)	760
FIPS code	06-36280
GNIS feature ID	1652726

Imperial is a city in Imperial County, California. Imperial is located 4 miles (6.4 km) north of El Centro. As of the 2006 census, the city had a population of 11,754. It is part of the El Centro metropolitan area. The City of Imperial is a bustling center in the Imperial Valley due to its central location in The Valley and proximity to Mexico. This makes Imperial an ideal location for industry, and business services.

Nearby recreation facilities transform the desert into a popular Valley tourist destination due to availability of different things to do. Three year-round golf courses which are operational year round are within minutes of Imperial. The sand dunes provide a place for campers and dune buggy enthusiasts. This regions is well known for its abundance of bird species such as dove, quail, ducks, pheasant and geese. Imperial is particularly noted for its friendly atmosphere and active community spirit. The city, is an excellent example of a well rounded cultural center.

Geography

Imperial is located at 32°50′51″N 115°34′10″W.

According to the United States Census Bureau, the city has a total area of 3.9 square miles (10.1 km²), all of it land.

Climate

Imperial has an arid desert climate. It is one of the hottest cities in the United States. In January, the normal high temperature is 70 degrees with a low of 42. In July, the normal high temperature is 110 degrees with a low of 82. Annual precipitation is around 3 inches.

History

Imperial was created by the Imperial Land Company and was named by George Chaffey. The first post office at Imperial opened in 1901. Imperial incorporated in 1904. The first Mayor of Imperial was Allison Peck.

Demographics

As of the census of 2006, there were 11,754 people, 2,308 households, and 1,911 families residing in the city. The population density was 1,932.2 people per square mile (746.5/km²). There were 2,385 housing units at an average density of 609.6/sq mi (235.5/km²). The racial makeup of the city was 58.53% White, 2.66% Black or African American, 0.75% Native American, 2.71% Asian, 0.17% Pacific Islander, 30.90% from other races, and 4.27% from two or more races. 61.10% of the population were Hispanic or Latino of any race.

There were 2,308 households out of which 53.9% had children under the age of 18 living with them, 65.9% were married couples living together, 13.0% had a female householder with no husband present, and 17.2% were non-families. 14.0% of all households were made up of individuals and 5.2% had someone living alone who was 65 years of age or older. The average household size was 3.26 and the average family size was 3.60.

In the city the population was spread out with 35.3% under the age of 18, 7.8% from 18 to 24, 33.8% from 25 to 44, 16.8% from 45 to 64, and 6.3% who were 65 years of age or older. The median age was 30 years. For every 100 females there were 96.8 males. For every 100 females age 18 and over, there were 91.5 males.

The median income for a household in the city was $49,451, and the median income for a family was $53,053. Males had a median income of $37,373 versus $27,778 for females. The per capita income for the city was $16,538. About 8.9% of families and 11.6% of the population were below the poverty line, including 15.2% of those under age 18 and 5.2% of those age 65 or over.

Politics

In the state legislature Imperial is located in the 40th Senate District, represented by Democrat Denise Moreno Ducheny, and in the 80th Assembly District, represented by Republican Bonnie Garcia. Federally, Imperial is located in California's 51st congressional district, which has a Cook PVI of D +7 and is represented by Democrat Bob Filner.

Events

Imperial has the annual California Mid-Winter Fair in February (formerly the Imperial County Fair) which receives over 100,000 visitors: either are locals, from nearby Mexicali, Baja California, Mexico and numerous "snowbirds" across Southern Cal. and the country (U.S.) temporarily reside in Imperial.

See also

- San Diego–Imperial, California
- El Centro Metropolitan Area

External links

- Imperial Chamber [1]
- City of Imperial Website [2]

Calipatria, California

City of Calipatria	
— City —	
Location in Imperial County and the state of California	
Coordinates: 33°07′32″N 115°30′51″W	
Country	United States
State	California
County	Imperial
Area	
- Total	3.7 sq mi (9.6 km^2)
- Land	3.7 sq mi (9.6 km^2)
- Water	0 sq mi (0 km^2)
Elevation	-177 ft (-54 m)
Population (2000)	
- Total	7289
- Density	1970/sq mi (759.3/km^2)
Time zone	Pacific (PST) (UTC-8)
- Summer (DST)	PDT (UTC-7)
ZIP code	92233
Area code(s)	760
FIPS code	06-09878
GNIS feature ID	1652681

Calipatria (formerly, **Date City**) is a city in Imperial County, California. Calipatria is located 23 miles (37 km) north of El Centro, It is part of the El Centro Metropolitan Area. The population was 7,289 at the 2000 census, including 4000 inmates at Calipatria State Prison. The community is located along State Route 111.

Geography

Calipatria is located at 33°07′32″N 115°30′51″W.

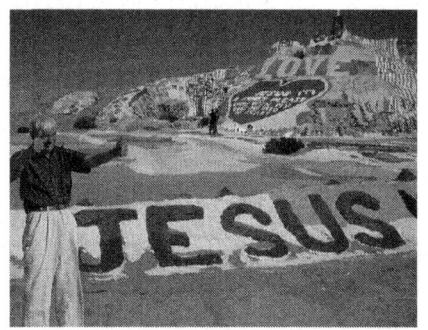

Leonard Knight at Salvation Mountain.

At elevation of 184 feet (56 m) below sea level, Calipatria is the lowest city in the western hemisphere. The city claims to have the "world's tallest flagpole" at 184 feet (56 m), so their American flag will always fly above sea level. However, this flagpole, in front of the local Chamber of Commerce, is far shorter than the 525 feet (160 m) in Kijŏng-dong, North Korea, the 430 feet (130 m) pole in Aqaba, Jordan, the 338 feet (103 m) pole in Sheboygan, Wisconsin or even the 200 feet (61 m) pole in Dorris, California, but it is probably the tallest flagpole in the Imperial Valley.

According to the United States Census Bureau, the city has a total area of 3.7 square miles (9.6 km²), all of it land.

History

The Imperial Valley Farm Lands Association founded the town as Date City in 1914. The first post office at Calipatria opened in 1914. Calipatria incorporated in 1919.

Demographics

As of the census of 2000, there were 7,289 people, 899 households, and 756 families residing in the city. The population density was 1,965.8 people per square mile (758.6/km²). There were 961 housing units at an average density of 259.2/sq mi (100.0/km²). The racial makeup of the city was 32.39% White, 21.32% Black or African American, 0.73% Native American, 0.63% Asian, 0.03% Pacific Islander, 42.65% from other races, and 2.25% from two or more races. 57.35% of the population were Hispanic or Latino of any race.

There were 899 households out of which 50.4% had children under the age of 18 living with them, 61.2% were married couples living together, 17.6% had a female householder with no husband present, and 15.8% were non-families. 14.1% of all households were made up of individuals and 5.6% had someone living alone who was 65 years of age or older. The average household size was 3.55 and the average family size was 3.90.

In the city the population was spread out with 16.3% under the age of 18, 12.3% from 18 to 24, 52.6% from 25 to 44, 15.0% from 45 to 64, and 3.8% who were 65 years of age or older. The median age was 33 years. For every 100 females there were 363.4 males. For every 100 females age 18 and over, there were 497.5 males.

The median income for a household in the city was $30,962, and the median income for a family was $31,302. Males had a median income of $31,350 versus $20,063 for females. The per capita income for the city was $13,970. About 20.4% of families and 24.2% of the population were below the poverty line, including 28.9% of those under age 18 and 17.8% of those age 65 or over.

Calipatria is one of the state's poorest cities in income per capita due to agricultural paychecks and a declined economy in the 1990s. Hispanics mostly of Mexican descent are three-fourths of the people (excluding the multiracial body of state prison convicts). The city was first called *Sante Patria* (as in "Saint of the Motherland") is founded by Irish American and Irish Mexican soldiers, who deserted both in the Mexican-American War (1850's) and from the Union and/or Confederate armies after the American Civil War (1860's) but Calipatria also has a large Arab population from Jordan, Lebanon and Syria, descendants of agriculture laborers in the 1920s. [*citation needed*]

Politics

In the state legislature Calipatria is located in the 40th Senate District, represented by Democrat Denise Moreno Ducheny, and in the 80th Assembly District, represented by Republican Bonnie Garcia. Federally, Calipatria is located in California's 51st congressional district, which has a Cook PVI of D +7 and is represented by Democrat Bob Filner.

Landmarks

Salvation Mountain is the notable tourist attraction in the north of Calipatria, near Slab City. Salvation Mountain is a small hill which is entirely covered in thousands of gallons of acrylic paint, straw, concrete, adobe. It was created by Leonard Knight to convey the message that "God Loves Everyone". Salvation Mountain was featured in the book *Into the Wild* and also in the 2007 movie of the same name. The video for *Fourth of July* by Shooter Jennings, is partially set at Salvation Mountain.

Sister cities

- Jericho, Palestinian Authority

See also

- San Diego–Imperial, California
- El Centro Metropolitan Area

External links

- Official Website [1]
- Map of the Sonoran Desert [2]

Holtville, California

City of Holtville	
— City —	
Holtville City Hall	
Location in Imperial County and the state of California	
Coordinates: 32°48′40″N 115°22′49″W	
Country	United States
State	California
County	Imperial
Area	
- Total	1.1 sq mi (3 km^2)
- Land	1.1 sq mi (3 km^2)
- Water	0 sq mi (0 km^2)
Elevation	-10 ft (-3 m)
Population (2000)	
- Total	5612
- Density	5101.8/sq mi (1870.7/km^2)
Time zone	Pacific (PST) (UTC-8)
- Summer (DST)	PDT (UTC-7)
ZIP code	92250
Area code(s)	760
FIPS code	06-34246
GNIS feature ID	1660761

Holtville (formerly, **Holton**) is a city in Imperial County, California. Holtville is located 10.5 miles (17 km) east of El Centro, The population was 5,612 at the 2000 census. It is part of the 'El Centro, California, Metropolitan Statistical Area'. City officials believed the population doubled in the last 6 years by 2007.

Holtville was famous in the 20th century with having the *Imperial Valley Carrot Festival* but was confused with the *Coachella Valley* from Bugs Bunny animated shorts in the 1940s when he reads the map seeking a Carrot Festival.

Geography

According to the United States Census Bureau, the city has a total area of 1.1 sq mi (2.8 km^2), all of it land.

History

The community started in 1903 as Holton. The first post office at Holtville was transferred from Eastside in 1904. Holtville incorporated in 1908. The name honors W.F. Holt, founder of the community.

Demographics

As of the census of 2000, there were 5,612 people, 1,564 households, and 1,340 families residing in the city. The population density was 4,920.8 people per square mile (1,900.7/km²). There were 1,617 housing units at an average density of 1,417.8/sq mi (547.7/km²). The racial makeup of the city was 54.37% White, 0.62% Black or African American, 0.84% Native American, 0.84% Asian, 0.07% Pacific Islander, 39.15% from other races, and 4.12% from two or more races. 73.84% of the population were Hispanic or Latino of any race.

There were 1,564 households out of which 52.1% had children under the age of 18 living with them, 64.9% were married couples living together, 16.5% had a female householder with no husband present, and 14.3% were non-families. 12.3% of all households were made up of individuals and 5.8% had someone living alone who was 65 years of age or older. The average household size was 3.51 and the average family size was 3.80.

In the city the population was spread out with 35.2% under the age of 18, 8.9% from 18 to 24, 26.5% from 25 to 44, 18.3% from 45 to 64, and 11.1% who were 65 years of age or older. The median age was 30 years. For every 100 females there were 94.1 males. For every 100 females age 18 and over, there were 89.4 males.

The median income for a household in the city was $36,318, and the median income for a family was $39,347. Males had a median income of $31,328 versus $26,477 for females. The per capita income for the city was $12,505. About 15.7% of families and 18.2% of the population were below the poverty line, including 23.2% of those under age 18 and 11.8% of those age 65 or over.

Politics

In the state legislature Holtville is located in the 40th Senate District, represented by Democrat Denise Moreno Ducheny, and in the 80th Assembly District, represented by Republican Bonnie Garcia. Federally, Holtville is located in California's 51st congressional district, which has a Cook PVI of D +7 and is represented by Democrat Bob Filner.

History was made during the election cycle of 2006, when voters elected Lisa Bianca Padilla, becoming the first female Hispanic candidate ever to win a seat on the city council.

General information

The city was founded by Swiss-German settlers in the 1880s often through the U.S.-Mexican border from Mexico. The construction of railroads in the 1890s, the All-American Canal in the late 1940s, U.S. Route 80 in the 1920s later converted to Interstate 8 in the 1970s and the North American Free Trade Agreement (NAFTA) economic boom in the 1990s brought more people to Holtville and the Imperial Valley.

The city of Holtville, which was originally called *Holton*, was founded in 1903 by W.F. Holt, and incorporated on June 20, 1908. The name was changed to Holtville due to a request by the Postal Service because the name Holton sounded too much like Colton, (in San Bernardino County), the regional headquarters of the Southern Pacific Railroad at the time.

The city lies on the northeast bank of the Alamo River formed by the floods of 1905-07 when the Colorado River break made the river's course turn west and filled the low-lying depression of water now the Salton Sea.

The old U.S. Route 80 once ran along Fifth Street through the center of town. A small obelisk in Holt Park, just north of Fifth Street, gives the distances to various points to the north, east and west. U.S. Route 80 has been decommissioned and made as County Route S80 in California. The portion in and near Holtville is now part of State Route 115.

Much of the east-west automobile traffic has been diverted to Interstate 8, about 2.5 miles to the south. Holtville is easily accessible through the Orchard Road interchange. The newly constructed State Route 7 connects Holtville with the factories and industrial areas of Mexicali, Baja California, Mexico.

The city was once joined by railroad to El Centro, but this line (nicknamed the "Holton Interurban"), and another railroad line going to the north, have been abandoned. The closure of the railroad station brought on economic decline to the town in the late 20th century.

The city's major civic event is the annual **Carrot Festival**, held in late January or early February. It usually features a parade, a carnival and other activities over a 10-day period. Holtville was famous in the mid 20th century with having the *Holtville* "Carrot Festival" but was confused with the "Coachella

Valley" name from Bugs Bunny animated shorts in the 1940s when he reads the map seeking a "Carrot Festival".

A weekly newspaper, *The Holtville Tribune*, is distributed by mail and newsstand in the Holtville area. Its circulation is about 3,750. The daily newspaper, the *Imperial Valley Press* in El Centro, has circulation at over 20,000.

The city was featured in Milton J. Silverman's bestselling novel "Open and Shut," which chronicled the true crime story of Norma Winters, a Holtville resident who contracted for the death of her husband during the summer of 1974.

Public safety

There is currently a call for the Holtville Police Department to be disbanded and replaced by a deputy of the Imperial County Sheriff's Department, due to the massive turnover of officers to other departments throughout California.

See also

- San Diego–Imperial, California
- El Centro Metropolitan Area

External links

- City of Holtville website [1]
- Holtville Chamber of Commerce [2]
- Map of Holtville and vicinity [3]

Attractions

Algodones Dunes

The **Algodones Dunes** is a large erg (sand dune field) located in the southeastern portion of the U.S. state of California, near the border with Arizona and the Mexican state of Baja California. The field is approximately 72 kilometers long by 10 kilometers wide (45 miles by 6 miles) and extends along a northwest-southeast line that correlates to the prevailing northerly and westerly wind directions. The name "Algodones Dunes" refers to the entire geographic feature, while the administrative designation for that portion managed by the Bureau of Land Management is the **Imperial Sand Dunes Recreation Area** (sometimes called the **Glamis Dunes**). The Algodones Dunes are split into many different sections. These sections include Glamis, Gordon's Well, Buttercup, Midway, and Patton's Valley. The Spanish word *algodones* translates to the English word *cotton*.

Algodones Dunes

Location

The dunes are located west of the Chocolate Mountains in Imperial County, and are crossed by Interstate Route 8 and State Route 78, which passes through the old train stop of Glamis at the eastern edge of the dune field. The northwestern end is located at 33°8′53″N 115°19′29″W about 18 km (11 miles) east of Calipatria, California, and the

The Algodones Dunes

southeastern end is located at 32°41′4″N 114°46′7″W near Los Algodones in Mexico about 10 km (six miles) west of Yuma, Arizona. The dunes are also now separated at the southern end by agricultural land (see accompanying photo) from the much more extensive Gran Desierto de Altar, to which they once were linked as an extreme peripheral "finger". The only significant human-made structures in the area are the All-American Canal that cuts across the southern portion from west to east and the Coachella Canal on the western edge.

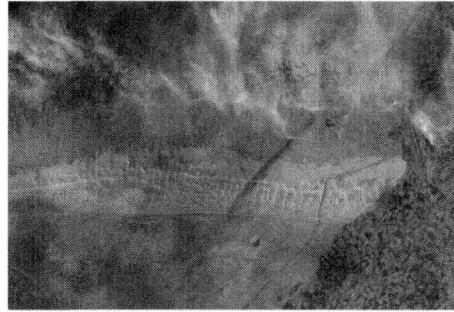

The Algodones Dunes from space. The Cargo Muchacho Mountains can be seen in the upper part of the image, beneath the clouds. A checkerboard pattern of farms in the Colorado River floodplain is visible on the Mexican side of the border (far right); the image is rotated about 50 degrees to the west.

History

Because the Colorado River flowed through very flat terrain, the course of the river varied over a wide area, being periodically diverted in one direction or another by silt deposits remaining after floods. Sometimes the river flowed into the Gulf of California, as it does today; other times it turned westward toward the Salton Sink. Each time the Salton Sink received the river flow, a large freshwater lake called Lake Cahuilla formed. The last Lake Cahuilla covered much of the Imperial, Coachella and Mexicali Valleys as late as 1450. The most popular theory holds that the Algodones Dunes were formed from windblown beach sands of Lake Cahuilla. The prevailing westerly and northwesterly winds carried the sand eastward from the old lake shore to their present location which continues to migrate southeast by approximately one foot per year.

The dunes have frequently been a barrier to human movement in the area. Foot travelers frequently diverted south into Mexico, and in 1877 the Southern Pacific Railroad was diverted north to avoid the dunes, but in 1915 Colonel Ed Fletcher built a wooden plank road across the dunes to prove that cars could cross the dunes and to connect San Diego with Yuma, Arizona. This trail eventually became part of Interstate 8. During World War II, the U.S. military conducted desert warfare training on the dunes, which were part of the California-Arizona Maneuver Area. People have been driving on the dunes for recreation almost since vehicles first reached the area, which may have been the proving ground for the first dune buggy, a modified Ford Model A. Off-road driving surged following World War II when surplus Jeeps became available to the public.

Current recreational use

Environmental protection groups (notably the Center for Biological Diversity) and off-highway vehicle advocacy groups (notably the American Sand Association) have filed numerous petitions and lawsuits to either restrict or re-open vehicular access to the dunes. Most of the dunes located north of State Route 78 are off-limits to vehicular traffic due to designation as the North Algodones Dunes Wilderness. The federal government protected these 25,818 acres (104 km²) in the early 1980s and closed them to vehicles as part of the 1994 California Desert Protection Act (Public Law 103-433). Much of the area south of this road remains open for off-highway vehicle use, though a lawsuit in 2000 closed over 49,000 acres (200 km²) to vehicular access, leaving about 40% of the recreation area open to vehicles. The site's large sand dunes are a preferred terrain for many off-road vehicle owners. Motorcycles, sandrails, ATVs, and 4-wheel-drive vehicles are commonly driven across the dunes. Open camping is permitted, and on major winter holidays, as many as 150,000 people can visit in a single weekend. These recreationalists bring an economic boom during the cooler months to the nearby towns of Brawley, California, Yuma, Arizona and El Centro, California.

Endemic species

As they are the largest dune ecosystem in the United States, there are many species which are endemic to the Algodones system, so the region overall is biologically unique on a global scale. The Algodones were once part of an even greater dune system that now resides primarily in the Mexican state of Sonora, with a few extensions also in southwestern Arizona, especially in the vicinity of Yuma. Accordingly, it is likely that many of the species presently known only from the Algodones also occur in the Gran Desierto de Altar in Mexico, but this is difficult to ascertain without biological surveys of the latter area.

- The perennial plant Peirson's Milkvetch aka the "Milk Weed" (*Astragalus magdalenae var. peirsonii*) is found in the Algodones and is listed as a threatened species under the U.S. Endangered Species Act and as an endangered species under the California Endangered Species Act. The plant germinates only during years of sufficient rainfall. During one such year, over 71,000 plants were found in the open areas of the dunes, and it is suspected at least that many more in the closed areas.

Among insects, there are dozens of species found only in Algodones or its neighboring areas, including:

- *Pseudocotalpa andrewsi* - (a scarab beetle)
- *Pseudocotalpa sonorica* - (a scarab beetle)
- *Anomala hardyorum* - (a scarab beetle)
- *Megasoma sleeperi* - (a scarab beetle)
- *Trigonoscuta rothi rothi* - (a weevil)
- *Trigonoscuta rothi algodones* - (a weevil)

- *Trigonoscuta rothi imperialis* - (a weevil)
- *Trigonoscuta rothi punctata* - (a weevil)
- *Lepismadora algodones* - (a buprestid beetle, the only member of its genus)
- *Agrilus harenus* - (a buprestid beetle)
- *Prasinalia imperialis* - (a buprestid beetle)
- *Microbembex elegans* - (a Sand wasp)
- *Stictiella villegasi* - (a Sand wasp)
- *Plenoculus* n. sp. - (a crabronid wasp)
- *Perdita glamis* - (an andrenid bee)
- *Perdita algodones* - (an andrenid bee)
- *Perdita frontalis* - (an andrenid bee)
- *Euparagia* n. sp. - (a vespid wasp)
- *Dasymutilla nocturna* - (a velvet ant)
- *Efferia macroxipha* - (a robber fly)

In August 2006, Federal wildlife officials decided not to list these species under the Endangered Species Act, due primarily to insufficient documentation of their distribution and phenology; biological survey work is planned to address this.

Movie setting

The dunes were used to film parts of *Road to Zanzibar*, *Flight of the Phoenix*, *Stargate*, *Resident Evil: Extinction* and the Tatooine scenes in *Return of the Jedi*.

External links

- Bureau of Land Management site for the Imperial Sand Dunes [1]
- Bureau of Land Management site for the North Algodones Dunes Wilderness [2]
- Center for Biological Diversity [3]
- North American Atlas 2006, pg. 17
- "Algodones Dunefield, California" [4]. NASA Earth Observatory. Retrieved 2006-05-01.
- Wilderness Net [5]
- Glamis Picture Gallery [6]
- Glamis Sand Dunes on Dirtopia [7]
- Imperial Sand Dunes on DuneGuide.com [8]
- Glamis Dunes website of information, forums and links [9]

<tr style="height:2px"><td><tr><td colspan=2 style="width:100%;padding:0px;;;" class="navbox-list navbox-odd">

National Forests

National Forests	Angeles · Cleveland · Eldorado · Inyo · Klamath · Lassen · Los Padres · Mendocino · Modoc · Plumas · San Bernardino · Sequoia · Shasta-Trinity · Sierra · Six Rivers · Stanislaus · Tahoe
National Wilderness Preservation System	Agua Tibia · Ansel Adams · Bucks Lake · Caribou · Carson-Iceberg · Castle Crags · Cucamonga · Desolation · Dick Smith · Dinkey Lakes · Emigrant · Golden Trout · Hoover · Inyo Mountains · Ishi · Jennie Lakes · John Muir · Kaiser · Marble Mountain · Mokelumne · Mount Shasta Wilderness · North Fork · San Gabriel · Sanhedrin · San Jacinto · San Rafael · Sespe · Siskuyou · Snow Mountain · South Fork Eel River · South Sierra · South Warner · Thousand Lakes · Trinity Alps · Ventana · Yolla Bolly-Middle Eel · Yuki
Other	Butte Valley National Grassland · Giant Sequoia National Monument · Santa Rosa and San Jacinto Mountains National Monument · Smith River National Recreation Area · Shasta-Trinity National Recreation Area

<tr style="height:2px"><td><tr><td colspan=2 style="width:100%;padding:0px;;;" class="navbox-list navbox-even">

State Forests

Boggs Mountain Demonstration · Ellen Pickett · Jackson Demonstration · Las Posadas · LaTour Demonstration · Mount Zion · Mountain Home Demonstration · Soquel Demonstration

<tr style="height:2px"><td><tr><td colspan=2 style="width:100%;padding:0px;;;" class="navbox-list navbox-odd">

National Wildlife Refuges

Antioch Dunes · Bitter Creek · Blue Ridge · Butte Sink · Castle Rock · Clear Lake · Coachella Valley · Colusa · Delevan · Don Edwards San Francisco Bay · Ellicott Slough · Farallon · Guadalupe-Nipomo Dunes · Hopper Mountain · Humboldt Bay · Kern · Lower Klamath · Marin Islands · Merced · Modoc · Pixley · Sacramento · Sacramento River · Salinas River · San Diego Bay · San Diego · San Joaquin River · San Luis · San Pablo Bay · Seal Beach · Sonny Bono Salton Sea · Stone Lakes · Sutter · Tijuana Slough · Tule Lake

<tr style="height:2px"><td><tr><td colspan=2 style="width:100%;padding:0px;;;" class="navbox-list navbox-even">

State Wildlife Areas

Wildlife AreasEcological ReservesMarine Protected Areas

Antelope Valley · Ash Creek · Bass Hill · Battle Creek · Big Lagoon · Big Sandy · Biscar · Butte Valley · Buttermilk Country · Cache Creek · Camp Cady · Cantara/Ney Springs · Cedar Roughs · Cinder Flats · Collins Eddy · Colusa Bypass · Coon Hollow · Cottonwood Creek · Crescent City Marsh · Crocker Meadows · Daugherty Hill · Decker Island · Doyle · Dutch Flat · Eastlker River · Eel

River · Elk Creek Wetlands · Elk River · Fay Slough · Feather River · Fitzhugh Creek · Fremont Weir · Grass Lake · Gray Lodge · Green Creek · Grizzly Island · Hallelujah Junction · Heenan Lake · Hill Slough · Hollenbeck Canyon · Honey Lake · Hope Valley · Horseshoe Ranch · Imperial · Indian Valley · Kelso Peak and Old Dad Mountains · Kinsman Flat · Knoxville · Laguna · Lake Berryessa · Lake Earl · Lake Sonoma · Little Panoche Reservoir · Los Banos · Lower Sherman Island · Mad River Slough · Marble Mountains · Mendota · Merrill's Landing · Miner Slough · Monache Meadows · Morro Bay · Moss Landing · Mouth of Cottonwood Creek · Napa-Sonoma Marshes · North Grasslands · O'Neill Forebay · Oroville · Petaluma Marsh · Pickel Meadow · Pine Creek · Point Edith · Putah Creek · Rector Reservoir · Red Lake · Rhode Island · Sacramento River · San Felipe Valley · San Jacinto · San Luis Obispo · San Luis Reservoir · San Pablo Bay · Santa Rosa · Shasta Valley · Silver Creek · Slinkard/Little Antelope · Smithneck Creek · South Fork · Spenceville · Surprise Valley · Sutter Bypass · Tehama · Truckee River · Upper Butte Basin · Volta · Warner Valley · Waukell Creek · West Hilmar · Westlker River · White Slough · Willow Creek · Yolo Bypass

Albany Mudflats · Alkali Sink · Allensworth · Atascadero Creek Marsh · Bair Island · Baldwin Lake · Batiquitos Lagoon · Blue Sky · Boden Canyon · Boggs Lake · Bolsa Chica · Bonny Doon · Buena Vista Lagoon · Butler Slough · Butte Creek Canyon · Butte Creek House · Buttonwillow · By Day Creek · Calhoun Cut · Canebrake · Carlsbad Highlands · Carmel Bay · Carrizo Canyon · Carrizo Plains · China Point · Clover Creek · Coachella Valley · Coal Canyon · Corte Madera Marsh · Crestridge · Dairy Mart Ponds · Dales Lake · Del Mar Landing · Elkhorn Slough · Estelle Mountain · Fall River Mills · Fish Slough · Fremont Valley · Goleta Slough · Indian Joe Spring · Kaweah · Kerman · King Clone · Laguna Laurel · Loch Lomond Vernal Pool · Lokern · Magnesia Spring · Marin Islands · Mattole River · McGinty Mountain · Morro Dunes · Morro Rock · Napa River · North Table Mountain · Oasis Spring · Panoche Hills · Peytonia Slough · Pine Hill · Piute Creek · Pleasant Valley · Point Lobos · Rancho Jamul · Redwood Shores · River Springs Lakes · Saline Valley · San Dieguito Lagoon · San Elijo Lagoon · San Felipe Creek · San Joaquin River · Santa Rosa Plateau · Springville · Stone Corral · Sycamore Canyon · Sycuan Peak · Thomes Creek · Tomales Bay · Upper Newport Bay · Watsonville Slough · West Mojave Desert · Woodbridge · Yaudanchi

Abalone Cove · Agua Hedionda Lagoon · Albany Mudflats · Anacapa · Anacapa · Año Nuevo · Asilomar · Atascadero Beach · Bair Island · Batiquitos Lagoon · Big Creek · Big Creek · Big Sycamore Canyon · Bodega · Bolsa Chica · Buena Vista Lagoon · Cambria · Cardiff and San Elijo · Carmel Bay · Carmel Pinnacles · Carrington Point · Catalina Marine Science Center · Corte Madera Marsh · Crystal Cove · Dana Point · Del Mar Landing · Doheny · Doheny · Duxbury Reef · Edward F. Ricketts · Elkhorn Slough · Elkhorn Slough · Encinitas · Estero de Limantour · Fagan Marsh · Farallon Islands · Farnsworth Bank · Fort Ross · Gerstle Cove · Goleta Slough · Greyhound Rock · Gull Island · Harris Point · Heisler Park · Hopkins · Irvine Coast · James V. Fitzgerald · Judith Rock · Julia Pfeiffer Burns · La Jolla · Laguna Beach · Lovers Cove (Catalina Island) · Lovers Point · MacKerricher · Manchester and Arena Rock · Marin Islands · Mia J. Tegner · Moro Cojo Slough · Morro Bay · Morro Bay · Morro Beach · Natural Bridges · Niguel · Pacific Grove Marine Gardens · Painted Cave · Peytonia Slough ·

Piedras Blancas · Piedras Blancas · Pismo · Pismo-Oceano Beach · Point Buchon · Point Buchon · Point Cabrillo · Point Fermin · Point Lobos · Point Reyes Headlands · Point Sur · Point Sur · Portuguese Ledge · Punta Gorda · Redwood Shores · Refugio · Richardson Rock · Robert E. Badham · Robert W. Crown · Russian Gulch · Russian River · Salt Point · San Diego-Scripps · San Dieguito Lagoon · San Elijo Lagoon · Santa Barbara Island · Scorpion · Skunk Point · Sonoma Coast · Soquel Canyon · South Laguna Beach · South Point · Tomales Bay · Upper Newport Bay · Van Damme · Vandenberg · White Rock (Cambria)

<tr style="height:2px"><td><tr><td colspan=2 style="width:100%;padding:0px;;;" class="navbox-list navbox-odd">

National Landscape Conservation System

National Monuments	California Coastal · Carrizo Plain · Santa Rosa and San Jacinto Mountains
National Conservation Areas	California Desert · King Range
Wilderness Areas	Argus Range · Big Maria Mountains · Bigelow Cholla Garden · Bighorn Mountain · Black Mountain · Bright Star · Bristol Mountains · Cadiz Dunes · Carrizo Gorge · Chemehuevi Mountains · Chimney Peak · Chuckwalla Mountains · Chumash · Cleghorn Lakes · Clipper Mountain · Coso Range · Coyote Mountains · Darwin Falls · Dead Mountains · Dick Smith · El Paso Mountains · Fish Creek Mountains · Funeral Mountains · Golden Valley · Grass Valley · Headwaters Forest Reserve · Hollow Hills · Ibex · Indian Pass · Inyo Mountains · Jacumba · Kelso Dunes · Kiavah · Kingston Range · Little Chuckwalla Mountains · Little Picacho · Machesna Mountain · Matilija · Malpais Mesa · Manly Peak · Mecca Hills · Mesquite · Newberry Mountains · Nopah Range · North Algodones Dunes · North Mesquite Mountains · Old Woman Mountains · Orocopia Mountains · Otay Mountain · Owens Peak · Pahrump Valley · Palen/McCoy · Palo Verde Mountains · Picacho Peak · Piper Mountain · Piute Mountains · Red Buttes · Resting Spring Range · Rice Valley · Riverside Mountains · Rodman Mountains · Sacatar Trail · Saddle Peak Hills · San Gorgonio · Santa Lucia · Santa Rosa · Sawtooth Mountains · Sespe · Sheephole Valley · South Nopah Range · Stateline · Stepladder Mountains · Surprise Canyon · Sylvania Mountains · Trilobite · Turtle Mountains · Whipple Mountains ·

<tr style="height:2px"><td><tr><td colspan=2 style="width:100%;padding:0px;;;" class="navbox-list navbox-even">

National Marine Sanctuaries

Channel Islands · Cordell Bank · Gulf of the Farallones · Monterey Bay

<tr style="height:2px"><td><tr><td colspan=2 style="width:100%;padding:0px;;;" class="navbox-list navbox-odd">

National Estuarine Research Reserves

Elkhorn Slough · San Francisco Bay · Tijuana River

<tr style="height:2px"><td><tr><td colspan=2 style="width:100%;padding:0px;;;" class="navbox-list navbox-even">

University of California Natural Reserve System

Año Nuevo Island · Bodega Marine · Box Springs · Boyd Deep Canyon Desert Research Center · Burns Piñon Ridge · Carpinteria Salt Marsh · Chickering American River · Coal Oil Point · Dawson Los Monos Canyon · Eagle Lake Field Station · Elliott Chaparral · Emerson Oaks · Fort Ord · Hastings · James San Jacinto Mountains · Jenny Pygmy Forest · Jepson Prairie · Kendall-Frost Mission Bay Marsh · Kenneth S. Norris Rancho Marino · Landels-Hill Big Creek · McLaughlin · Motte Rimrock · Quail Ridge · Sagehen Creek Field Station · San Joaquin Freshwater Marsh · Santa Cruz Island · Scripps Coastal · Sedgwick · Stebbins Cold Canyon · Stunt Ranch Santa Monica Mountains · Sweeney Granite Mountains Desert Research Center · Valentine Eastern Sierra · Younger Lagoon

<tr style="height:2px;"><td><tr><td class="navbox-abovebelow" style=";background:#ffc94b;" colspan="2">

Heritage registers: World Heritage Sites · World Network of Biosphere Reserves · National Register of Historic Places · National Historic Landmarks · National Natural Landmarks · California Historical Landmarks · California Points of Historical Interest · California Register of Historical Resources

Salvation Mountain

Geographical coordinates: 33°15′14.9″N 115°28′21.4″W

Salvation Mountain is a colorful art installation covering much of a small hill north of Calipatria, California, near Slab City and just several miles from the Salton Sea. It is made from adobe, straw, and thousands of gallons of paint. It was created by Leonard Knight to convey the message that "God Loves Everyone." Knight refused substantial donations of money and labor from supporters who wished to modify his message of universal love to favor or disfavor particular groups.[*citation needed*]

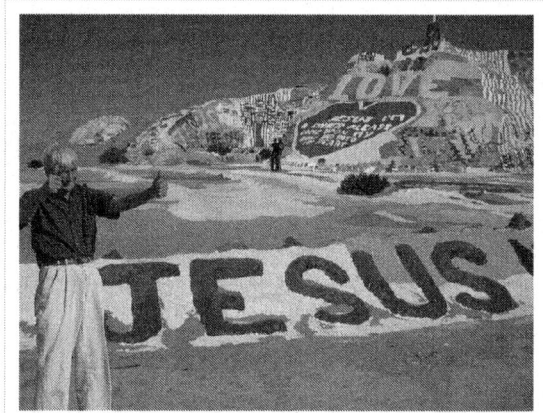

Leonard Knight at Salvation Mountain.

Steps cut into the side of the hill lead to the summit, which is topped by a cross. Salvation Mountain also features many large straw bale and adobe walls supported by a matrix of logs enclosing several cave-like spaces. Knight lives full-time at the site in a small cabin mounted on the rear of a 1930s-vintage Chevrolet two-ton truck. Like Salvation Mountain, Knight's "Salvation Truck" and a collection of other vehicles and machinery are entirely covered with paint and Biblical quotes. He estimates that more than 100,000 gallons of paint have gone into the creation of the mountain and that every California-based paint manufacturer has donated paint to the project.

Friendly and accessible, Leonard welcomes visitors to Slab City and Salvation Mountain and gladly accepts donations of both labor and acrylic paint. Once labeled an environmental hazard, the hill was threatened with removal by Imperial County. In recent years, the furor seems to have died down and the project has been likened to an epic work of folk art comparable to the Watts Towers. Although the project is an unauthorized one on state land, Salvation Mountain was placed under protection in 2002 when Senator Barbara Boxer entered it into the Congressional Record as a national treasure.

In popular culture

Salvation Mountain was featured in the 2007 film *Into the Wild*, as well as several documentaries including *Plagues & Pleasures on the Salton Sea*, *Desertopia*, and *Mountain*.

It can also be seen on the back cover photographs of the Kyuss albums *...And The Circus Leaves Town* and *Muchas Gracias: The Best of Kyuss*, and on the Switchfoot Album *Hello Hurricane*.

External links

- Salvation Mountain [1] - Official Website
- Documentary - "Plagues & Pleasures on the Salton Sea" [2]
- Video Tour of Salvation Mountain with Leonard Knight [3] at Youtube.com
- Salvation Mountain [4] on Google Maps
- Walkable virtual tour and treasure hunt [5] on Snubble.com
- Extensive photo essay on Salvation Mountain [6]: by National Geographic photographer Aaron Huey
- Portraits of Leonard Knight [7]: by photographer Jace Rivers
- Portraits of Leonard Knight [8]: by photographer Brooks Reynolds on cover and inside Mountains magazine issue 1

Anza-Borrego Desert State Park

Anza-Borrego Desert State Park	
IUCN Category III (Natural Monument)	
 Desert view from Font's Point	
Location	San Diego County, Imperial County, Riverside County, California, United States
Nearest city	Borrego Springs - Julian
Coordinates	33°15′23″N 116°23′57″W
Area	600,000 acres (2,420 km²)
Governing body	California State Parks
Official website [1]	

Anza-Borrego Desert State Park is a desert nature reserve, primarily within the Colorado Desert region of eastern San Diego County, and reaching into Imperial and Riverside Counties, in Southern California, the United States.

Geography

Anza-Borrego Desert State Park is named after 18th century Spanish explorer Juan Bautista de Anza and from the Spanish word *Borrego* meaning Bighorn sheep. With 600000 acres (2400 km^2) that include one fifth of San Diego County within its borders,

Panoramic view from Font's Point westward over Borrego Valley to the Laguna Mountains.

Anza-Borrego is the largest in State Park in California; and after New York's Adirondack Park it's the second largest one in all the continental United States.

Anza-Borrego is around a two-hour drive: northeast from San Diego, southeast from Riverside or Irvine, and south from Palm Springs. The Park is an anchor in the Mojave and Colorado Deserts Biosphere Reserve, and adjacent to the Santa Rosa and San Jacinto Mountains National Monument.

Visiting

Anza-Borrego Desert State Park includes 500-mile (800 km) of dirt roads, twelve designated wilderness area, and 110 miles (180 km) of hiking trails to provide visitors with many opportunities to experience the Park's unique version of the Colorado Desert environs. Park information and maps, interpretive events and displays, and listening devices for the hearing impaired, are all available in the Visitor Center.

Vista of the Anza Borrego desert landscape.

Anza-Borrego Desert State Park has wi-fi access in various sections of the park, as do fifty five other California State Parks.

Many visitors approach Anza-Borrego from the east-Coachella Valley side via California County Routes S22 and S78. Visitors can also approach from the west-Pacific Ocean side via California County Routes S79 or S67 and add experiences of passing through through the high and forested Laguna Mountains, such as in Cuyamaca Rancho State Park. These highways climb from the coast to

2400-foot (730 m) high then descend 2000-foot (610 m) down into the Borrego Valley in the center of the Park. This great bowl of the Anza-Borrego desert is surrounded by mountains, with the Vallecito Mountains southward and the highest Santa Rosa Mountains to the north. They are in the Park's wilderness area, without paved roads and with the only year-round creeks in Anza-Borrego.

Flora and fauna

See also: Category: Flora of the California desert regions
and also: Category: Fauna of the Colorado Desert

The habitats of Anza-Borrego Desert State Park are primarily within the Colorado Desert ecosystem of the Sonoran Desert ecoregion. The higher extreme northern and eastern sections in the Peninsular Ranges are in the California montane chaparral and woodlands ecoregion.

The park features: bajadas and desert washes; rock formations and colorful badlands, vast arid landscapes and dramatic mountains. The bajadas are predominantly creosote bush-bur sage with Creosote bush (*Larrea tridentata*) and the palo verde-cactus shrub ecosystems with the Palo Verde tree (*Parkinsonia microphylla*), cacti, and Ocotillo. In the washes, Colorado/Sonoran microphylla woodlands can be found. These woodlands include such plants as Smoke Tree (*Psorothamnus spinosus*), Honey Mesquite (*Prosopis velutina*), and Catclaw (*Acacia greggii*).

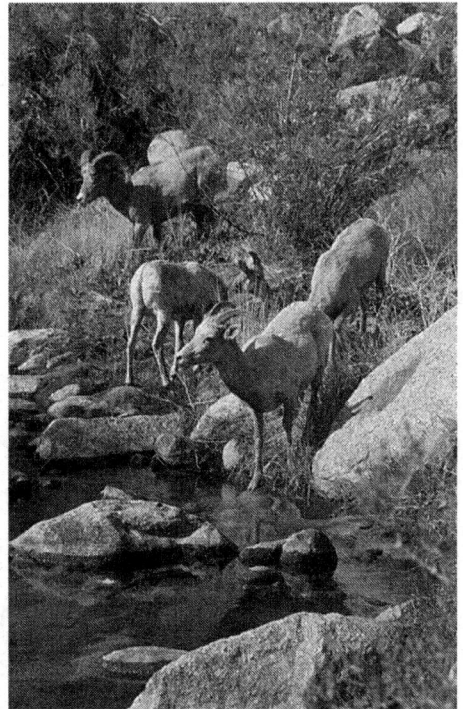

Desert Bighorn Sheep at Palm Canyon Oasis.

Anza Borrego has natural springs and oases with the state's only native palm, the endangered California fan palm (*Washingtonia filifera*). Seasonal wildflower displays can be stunning in any plant community association in throughout the Park. The high-county to the north and east has Closed-cone pine forests, Manzanitas, and Oak woodlands.

The oases are prolific with wildlife of all types of fauna, especially for bird-watching. Throughout the Park visitors may see Kit foxes, Mule deer, Coyotes, Greater roadrunners, Golden eagles, Black-tailed jackrabbits, Ground squirrels, Kangaroo rats, Quail, and Prairie falcons. In the reptile class Desert iguanas, Chuckwallas and the Red diamond rattlesnake can be seen - with care.

Desert Bighorn Sheep

Some areas of Anza-Borrego Park are habitat for the Peninsular bighorn sheep, often called Desert Bighorn Sheep. Few park visitors see them, and the sheep are justly wary. A patient few observers each year see and count this endangered species, to study the population, and to monitor its current decline from human overpopulation encroachment.

Geology and paleontology

The expanses of Anza-Borrego's eroded badlands also provide a different view into the region's long vanished tropical past. The inland of southeastern California was not always a desert. Paleontology, the study of the fossilized remains of ancient life, is the key to understanding and engaging this prehistoric world. Anza-Borrego has an exceptional fossil record; and include preserved plants, a variety of invertebrate shells, animal tracks and an vast array of bones and teeth. Most Anza-Borrego fossils date from six million to under a half million years in age, or about 60 million years after the last dinosaur age ended.

Geology

Anza-Borrego Desert lies in a unique geologic setting along the western margin of the Salton Trough. This major topographic depression with the Salton Sink having elevations of 200-foot (61 m) below sea level, forms the northernmost end of an active rift valley and a geological continental plate boundary. The Trough extends north from the Sea of Cortez (Gulf of California) to San Gorgonio Pass, and from the eastern rim of the Peninsular Ranges eastward to the San Andreas Fault Zone along the far side of the Coachella Valley. Over the past 7 million years, a relatively complete geologic record of

Anza-Borrego rock outcrop and flora

over 20000-foot (6100 m) of fossil bearing sediment has been deposited within the Park along the rift valley's western margin. Here, paleontological remains are widespread and exceedingly diverse, and are found scattered over hundreds of square miles of eroded badlands terrain extending south from the Santa Rosa Mountains Range into northern Baja California in Mexico.

Both marine and terrestrial environments are represented by this long and rich fossil record. Six million years ago the ancestral Gulf of California filled the Salton Trough, extending northward past what would become the city of Palm Springs. These tropical waters supported a profusion of both large and small marine organisms. Through time, the sea gave way as an immense volume of sediment eroded during the formation of the Grand Canyon spilled into the Salton Trough. Bit-by-bit, the ancestral Colorado River built a massive river delta across the sea way. Fossil hard woods from the deltaic sands and associated coastal plain deposits suggest that the region received three times as much rainfall as present times.

The Anza-Borrego region gradually changed from a predominately marine environment in to a system of interrelated terrestrial habitats. North of the Colorado River Delta and intermittently fed by the River, a sequence of lakes and playa lakes has persisted for over 3 million years. At the same time, sediments eroded from the growing Santa Rosa Mountains and other Peninsular Ranges to spread east into the Trough. It is these sediments that provide an almost unbroken terrestrial fossil record, ending only a half million years ago. Here, the deposits of ancient streams and rivers trapped the remains of wildlife that inhabited a vast brushland savannah laced with riparian woodlands.

Fossils

This record of changing environments and habitats includes over 550 types of fossil plants and animals, ranging from preserved microscopic plant pollen and algae spores to baleen whale bones and mammoth skeletons. Many of the species are extinct and some are known only from fossil remains recovered from this Park. Combined with a long and complete sedimentary depositional sequence, these diverse fossil assemblages are an unparalleled paleontologic resource of international importance. Both the Pliocene-Pleistocene Epoch boundary and the Blancan-Irvingtonian North American Land Mammal Ages boundary fall within the long geological record from the Anza-Borrego Desert. Environmental changes associated with these geological time divisions are probably better tracked by fossils from Anza-Borrego than in any other North American continental platform strata. These changes herald the beginning of the Ice Ages, and the strata contain fossil clues to the origin and development of modern southwestern desert landscapes.

The first fossils, marine shells from the ancient Sea of Cortez and fresh water shells from a prehistoric era Lake Cahuilla, precursor of present day Salton Sea, were collected and described by William Blake in 1853. Blake was the geologist and mineralogist for the Pacific Railroad Surveys commissioned by Congress and President Franklin Pierce to find a railway route to the Pacific. It was Blake who first named this region the Colorado Desert.

Marine period

Since the late 19th century, numerous scientific studies and published papers have centered on the marine organisms that inhabited the ancient Sea of Cortez. Fossil assemblages from the classic 'Imperial Formation' include calcareous nanoplankton and dinoflagellates, foraminifera, corals, polychaetes, clams, gastropods, sea urchins, and sand dollars, and crabs and shrimp. The deposits also yield the remains of marine vertebrates such as sharks and rays, bony fish, baleen whale, walrus, and dugong.

Pre-Colombian rock art in the Indian Hill archeological area.

Marine environments such as outer and inner shelf, platform reef, and near shore beach and lagoon are all represented within the 'Imperial Formation.' As the sea shallowed, estuarine and brackish marine conditions prevailed, typified by thick channel deposits of oyster and pecten shell coquina that now form the "Elephant Knees" along Fish Creek. Many of the marine fossils are closely related to forms from the Caribbean Sea. They document a time before the isthmus of Panama formed, when the warm Gulf Stream of the western Atlantic invaded eastern Pacific Ocean waters.

Terrestrial period

As North and South America connected about 3 million years ago, terrestrial faunal north-south migrations began on a continental scale called the Great American Biotic Interchange, and are present in Anza-Borrego's fossils. Animals like giant ground sloths and porcupines made their first appearance in North America at this time.

The oldest terrestrial vertebrate fossils from the Colorado Desert predate the late Miocene invasion of the Sea of Cortez. These very rare fossils, which include a gomphothere (elephant-like mammal), rodent, felid and small camelid, and were collected from 10-12 million year old riverine and near shore lake deposits. However, the most significant and abundant vertebrate fossils have been recovered from the latest Miocene through late-Pleistocene riverine and flood plane deposits of the Palm Spring Formation in the Vallecito and Fish Creek Badlands and Ocotillo Conglomerate exposed in the Borrego Badlands. These fossil assemblages occur in a 3.5 million year long uninterrupted stratigraphic sequence that has been dated using horizons of volcanic ash and paleomagnetic methods.

The bestiary for this savannah landscape reads like a "who's-who" for some of the most unique creatures to inhabit North America - animals such as:

Geochelone, a giant bathtub-sized tortoise; *Aiolornis incredibilis*, the largest flying bird of the northern hemisphere, with 17-foot (5.2 m) wing span; *Paramylodon*, *Megalonyx* and *Nothrotheriops*, giant ground sloths, some with bony armor within their skin; *Pewelagus*, a very small rabbit (paleontologists can name with a sense of humor); *Borophagus*, a hyena-like dog; *Acrtodus*, a giant short-faced bear;

Smilodon, a sabertoothed cat; *Miracinonyx*, the North American cheetah; *Mammuthus imperator*, the largest known mammoth; *Tapirus*, an extinct tapir; *Equus enormis* and *Equus scotti*, two species of extinct Pleistocene horse; *Gigantocamelus* a giant camel; and *Capromeryx*, the dwarf pronghorn.

Future

Although paleontological exploration of Anza-Borrego Desert State Park has stepped firmly into the 21st century with the application of GIS and computer assisted analyses to field surveys and resource management, many questions still remain as new fossils are discovered. Expanding the detail and clarity of the paleontological view of the region's past and improving understanding of its significance is ongoing.

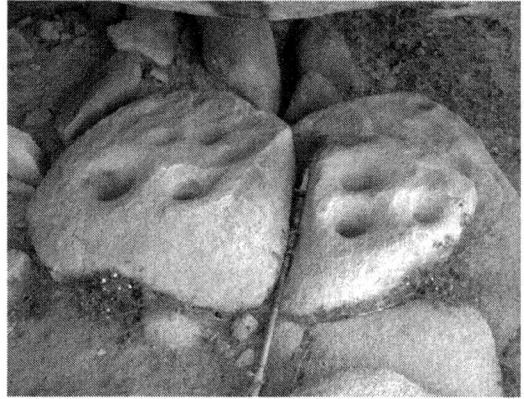

Morteros, bedrock mortar grinding holes, in the Indian Hill area.

Native Americans

The Native Americans of the Anza-Borrego mountains and deserts included the Cahuilla, Cupeño, Diegueño, and Kumeyaay Indian tribes. It was the homeland of these peoples for thousands of years, and their artists created petroglyph and pictogram "Rock art" expressing their cultures.

Gallery

Flora and Fauna of Anza-Borrego Desert Park

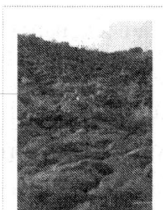

Penninsular Bighorn Sheep in Anza-Borrego.

An Ocotillo plant common in Anza-Borrego.

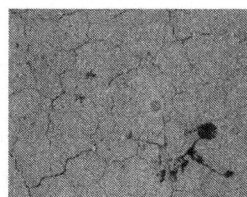

A lone Desert Marigold pushes its way through the cracked, sun hardened desert after a rare and substantial rainfall (Spring 2004).

Common Chuckwalla, *Sauromalus ater*. Observed during a hike up Palm Canyon.

Park interpretive associations

Anza-Borrego Foundation State Park Store and Visitor Center

The Anza-Borrego Foundation [2] is the Co-operating Association for the State Park it operates all sales at the State Park Visitor Center, 200 Palm Canyon Dr., Borrego Springs, CA 92004, and State Park Store, 587 Palm Canyon Drive Suite 110, The Mall, Borrego Springs, CA 92004. Anza-Borrego Institute [1] offers in depth field programs, fifth grade environmental camp, citizen science research, and Parks Online Resources for Teachers and Students.

Anza-Borrego Foundation

The Anza-Borrego Foundation (ABF) [2], founded in 1967, is a non-profit educational organization and is the sole cooperating association of Anza-Borrego Desert State Park. The Anza-Borrego Institute, the education arm of ABF, provides in-depth educational courses to more than 1,300 visitors each year. ABF's mission is to protect and preserve the natural landscapes, wildlife habitat, and cultural heritage of Anza-Borrego Desert State Park for the benefit and enjoyment of present and future generations.

Borrego Desert Nature Center

The Anza-Borrego Desert Natural History Association operates the Borrego Desert Nature Center [3] in Borrego Springs. The nature center offers educational, environmental, and recreational programs for all ages including desert tours, guided hikes, and lectures.

Borrego Springs Chamber of Commerce

Borrego Springs Chamber of Commerce Visitor Center; offers the Comprehensive Guide to Borrego Springs community [4]; 786 Palm Canyon Drive, Borrego Springs,CA 92004.

See also

Articles

- Ocotillo Wells, California
- Santa Rosa and San Jacinto Mountains National Monument
- Mojave and Colorado Deserts Biosphere Reserve
  - Man and the Biosphere Programme
  - World Network of Biosphere Reserves—World Network of Biosphere Reserves in Europe and North America

Index links

- Category: Fauna of the Sonoran Desert
- Category: Geography of the Colorado Desert
- Category: Mountain ranges of the Colorado Desert
- Category: Protected areas of the Colorado Desert
- Category: Native American history of California

References

Reference Books

- C. Michael Hogan. 2009. *California Fan Palm: Washingtonia filifera*, GlobalTwitcher.com, ed. Nicklas Stromberg [5]
- George T. Jefferson and Lowell Lindsay. 2006. *Fossil Treasures of the Anza-Borrego Desert* (Sunbelt Publications, San Diego). ISBN 0932653502

Further reading

- Robin Halford. 2005. *Hiking in Anza-Borrego Desert: Over 100 Half-Day Hikes* (Anza Borrego Desert Natural History Association, Borrego Springs). ISBN 091080513X
- Diana Lindsay, 2001. *Anza-Borrego A to Z: People, Places, and Things* (Sunbelt Publications, San Diego). ISBN 0932653421
- Lowell Lindsay and Lindsay, Diana. 2006. *The Anza-Borrego Desert Region: A Guide to the State Park and Adjacent Areas of the Western Colorado Desert. Fifth Edition* (Wilderness Press, Berkeley). ISBN 0899974007
- George T. Jefferson and Lowell Lindsay. 2006. *Fossil Treasures of the Anza-Borrego Desert* (Sunbelt Publications, San Diego). ISBN 0932653502
- *Serenity (film)* - location shooting in the park for the 2005 feature film shows the environs.

External links

- Official **Anza-Borrego Desert State Park website** [1]
- ABDSP.org Extensive Anza-Borrego information website [6]
- Anza-Borrego Foundation and Institute [7]
- Anza-Borrego Desert Natural History Association [8]
- Paleontology Society of the Anza-Borrego Desert State Park [9]
- Encyclopaedia Britannica: Anza-Borrego Desert State Park [10]
- Anza-Borrego on Dirtopia [11]
- Anza-Borrego Desert State Park — "A Tribute: [12]
- Extensive hiking in Anza-Borrego [13]

- official U.S. National Park Service **Juan Bautista de Anza National Historic Trail** website [14] - *Coyote Canyon*

<tr style="height:2px"><td><tr><td colspan=2 style="width:100%;padding:0px;;;" class="navbox-list navbox-odd">

National Forests

National Forests	Angeles · Cleveland · Eldorado · Inyo · Klamath · Lassen · Los Padres · Mendocino · Modoc · Plumas · San Bernardino · Sequoia · Shasta-Trinity · Sierra · Six Rivers · Stanislaus · Tahoe
National Wilderness Preservation System	Agua Tibia · Ansel Adams · Bucks Lake · Caribou · Carson-Iceberg · Castle Crags · Cucamonga · Desolation · Dick Smith · Dinkey Lakes · Emigrant · Golden Trout · Hoover · Inyo Mountains · Ishi · Jennie Lakes · John Muir · Kaiser · Marble Mountain · Mokelumne · Mount Shasta Wilderness · North Fork · San Gabriel · Sanhedrin · San Jacinto · San Rafael · Sespe · Siskuyou · Snow Mountain · South Fork Eel River · South Sierra · South Warner · Thousand Lakes · Trinity Alps · Ventana · Yolla Bolly-Middle Eel · Yuki
Other	Butte Valley National Grassland · Giant Sequoia National Monument · Santa Rosa and San Jacinto Mountains National Monument · Smith River National Recreation Area · Shasta-Trinity National Recreation Area

<tr style="height:2px"><td><tr><td colspan=2 style="width:100%;padding:0px;;;" class="navbox-list navbox-even">

State Forests

Boggs Mountain Demonstration · Ellen Pickett · Jackson Demonstration · Las Posadas · LaTour Demonstration · Mount Zion · Mountain Home Demonstration · Soquel Demonstration

<tr style="height:2px"><td><tr><td colspan=2 style="width:100%;padding:0px;;;" class="navbox-list navbox-odd">

National Wildlife Refuges

Antioch Dunes · Bitter Creek · Blue Ridge · Butte Sink · Castle Rock · Clear Lake · Coachella Valley · Colusa · Delevan · Don Edwards San Francisco Bay · Ellicott Slough · Farallon · Guadalupe-Nipomo Dunes · Hopper Mountain · Humboldt Bay · Kern · Lower Klamath · Marin Islands · Merced · Modoc · Pixley · Sacramento · Sacramento River · Salinas River · San Diego Bay · San Diego · San Joaquin River · San Luis · San Pablo Bay · Seal Beach · Sonny Bono Salton Sea · Stone Lakes · Sutter · Tijuana Slough · Tule Lake

<tr style="height:2px"><td><tr><td colspan=2 style="width:100%;padding:0px;;;" class="navbox-list navbox-even">

State Wildlife Areas

Wildlife AreasEcological ReservesMarine Protected Areas

Antelope Valley · Ash Creek · Bass Hill · Battle Creek · Big Lagoon · Big Sandy · Biscar · Butte Valley · Buttermilk Country · Cache Creek · Camp Cady · Cantara/Ney Springs · Cedar Roughs · Cinder Flats · Collins Eddy · Colusa Bypass · Coon Hollow · Cottonwood Creek · Crescent City Marsh · Crocker Meadows · Daugherty Hill · Decker Island · Doyle · Dutch Flat · Eastlker River · Eel River · Elk Creek Wetlands · Elk River · Fay Slough · Feather River · Fitzhugh Creek · Fremont Weir · Grass Lake · Gray Lodge · Green Creek · Grizzly Island · Hallelujah Junction · Heenan Lake · Hill Slough · Hollenbeck Canyon · Honey Lake · Hope Valley · Horseshoe Ranch · Imperial · Indian Valley · Kelso Peak and Old Dad Mountains · Kinsman Flat · Knoxville · Laguna · Lake Berryessa · Lake Earl · Lake Sonoma · Little Panoche Reservoir · Los Banos · Lower Sherman Island · Mad River Slough · Marble Mountains · Mendota · Merrill's Landing · Miner Slough · Monache Meadows · Morro Bay · Moss Landing · Mouth of Cottonwood Creek · Napa-Sonoma Marshes · North Grasslands · O'Neill Forebay · Oroville · Petaluma Marsh · Pickel Meadow · Pine Creek · Point Edith · Putah Creek · Rector Reservoir · Red Lake · Rhode Island · Sacramento River · San Felipe Valley · San Jacinto · San Luis Obispo · San Luis Reservoir · San Pablo Bay · Santa Rosa · Shasta Valley · Silver Creek · Slinkard/Little Antelope · Smithneck Creek · South Fork · Spenceville · Surprise Valley · Sutter Bypass · Tehama · Truckee River · Upper Butte Basin · Volta · Warner Valley · Waukell Creek · West Hilmar · Westlker River · White Slough · Willow Creek · Yolo Bypass

Albany Mudflats · Alkali Sink · Allensworth · Atascadero Creek Marsh · Bair Island · Baldwin Lake · Batiquitos Lagoon · Blue Sky · Boden Canyon · Boggs Lake · Bolsa Chica · Bonny Doon · Buena Vista Lagoon · Butler Slough · Butte Creek Canyon · Butte Creek House · Buttonwillow · By Day Creek · Calhoun Cut · Canebrake · Carlsbad Highlands · Carmel Bay · Carrizo Canyon · Carrizo Plains · China Point · Clover Creek · Coachella Valley · Coal Canyon · Corte Madera Marsh · Crestridge · Dairy Mart Ponds · Dales Lake · Del Mar Landing · Elkhorn Slough · Estelle Mountain · Fall River Mills · Fish Slough · Fremont Valley · Goleta Slough · Indian Joe Spring · Kaweah · Kerman · King Clone · Laguna Laurel · Loch Lomond Vernal Pool · Lokern · Magnesia Spring · Marin Islands · Mattole River · McGinty Mountain · Morro Dunes · Morro Rock · Napa River · North Table Mountain · Oasis Spring · Panoche Hills · Peytonia Slough · Pine Hill · Piute Creek · Pleasant Valley · Point Lobos · Rancho Jamul · Redwood Shores · River Springs Lakes · Saline Valley · San Dieguito Lagoon · San Elijo Lagoon · San Felipe Creek · San Joaquin River · Santa Rosa Plateau · Springville · Stone Corral · Sycamore Canyon · Sycuan Peak · Thomes Creek · Tomales Bay · Upper Newport Bay · Watsonville Slough · West Mojave Desert · Woodbridge · Yaudanchi

Abalone Cove · Agua Hedionda Lagoon · Albany Mudflats · Anacapa · Anacapa · Año Nuevo · Asilomar · Atascadero Beach · Bair Island · Batiquitos Lagoon · Big Creek · Big Creek · Big Sycamore Canyon · Bodega · Bolsa Chica · Buena Vista Lagoon · Cambria · Cardiff and San Elijo · Carmel Bay · Carmel Pinnacles · Carrington Point · Catalina Marine Science Center · Corte Madera Marsh · Crystal Cove · Dana Point · Del Mar Landing · Doheny · Doheny · Duxbury Reef · Edward F. Ricketts · Elkhorn Slough · Elkhorn Slough · Encinitas · Estero de Limantour · Fagan Marsh · Farallon Islands · Farnsworth Bank · Fort Ross · Gerstle Cove · Goleta Slough · Greyhound Rock · Gull Island · Harris

Point · Heisler Park · Hopkins · Irvine Coast · James V. Fitzgerald · Judith Rock · Julia Pfeiffer Burns · La Jolla · Laguna Beach · Lovers Cove (Catalina Island) · Lovers Point · MacKerricher · Manchester and Arena Rock · Marin Islands · Mia J. Tegner · Moro Cojo Slough · Morro Bay · Morro Bay · Morro Beach · Natural Bridges · Niguel · Pacific Grove Marine Gardens · Painted Cave · Peytonia Slough · Piedras Blancas · Piedras Blancas · Pismo · Pismo-Oceano Beach · Point Buchon · Point Buchon · Point Cabrillo · Point Fermin · Point Lobos · Point Reyes Headlands · Point Sur · Point Sur · Portuguese Ledge · Punta Gorda · Redwood Shores · Refugio · Richardson Rock · Robert E. Badham · Robert W. Crown · Russian Gulch · Russian River · Salt Point · San Diego-Scripps · San Dieguito Lagoon · San Elijo Lagoon · Santa Barbara Island · Scorpion · Skunk Point · Sonoma Coast · Soquel Canyon · South Laguna Beach · South Point · Tomales Bay · Upper Newport Bay · Van Damme · Vandenberg · White Rock (Cambria)

<tr style="height:2px"><td><tr><td colspan=2 style="width:100%;padding:0px;;;" class="navbox-list navbox-odd">

National Landscape Conservation System

National Monuments	California Coastal · Carrizo Plain · Santa Rosa and San Jacinto Mountains
National Conservation Areas	California Desert · King Range
Wilderness Areas	Argus Range · Big Maria Mountains · Bigelow Cholla Garden · Bighorn Mountain · Black Mountain · Bright Star · Bristol Mountains · Cadiz Dunes · Carrizo Gorge · Chemehuevi Mountains · Chimney Peak · Chuckwalla Mountains · Chumash · Cleghorn Lakes · Clipper Mountain · Coso Range · Coyote Mountains · Darwin Falls · Dead Mountains · Dick Smith · El Paso Mountains · Fish Creek Mountains · Funeral Mountains · Golden Valley · Grass Valley · Headwaters Forest Reserve · Hollow Hills · Ibex · Indian Pass · Inyo Mountains · Jacumba · Kelso Dunes · Kiavah · Kingston Range · Little Chuckwalla Mountains · Little Picacho · Machesna Mountain · Matilija · Malpais Mesa · Manly Peak · Mecca Hills · Mesquite · Newberry Mountains · Nopah Range · North Algodones Dunes · North Mesquite Mountains · Old Woman Mountains · Orocopia Mountains · Otay Mountain · Owens Peak · Pahrump Valley · Palen/McCoy · Palo Verde Mountains · Picacho Peak · Piper Mountain · Piute Mountains · Red Buttes · Resting Spring Range · Rice Valley · Riverside Mountains · Rodman Mountains · Sacatar Trail · Saddle Peak Hills · San Gorgonio · Santa Lucia · Santa Rosa · Sawtooth Mountains · Sespe · Sheephole Valley · South Nopah Range · Stateline · Stepladder Mountains · Surprise Canyon · Sylvania Mountains · Trilobite · Turtle Mountains · Whipple Mountains ·

<tr style="height:2px"><td><tr><td colspan=2 style="width:100%;padding:0px;;;" class="navbox-list navbox-even">

National Marine Sanctuaries

Channel Islands · Cordell Bank · Gulf of the Farallones · Monterey Bay

<tr style="height:2px"><td><tr><td colspan=2 style="width:100%;padding:0px;;;" class="navbox-list navbox-odd">

National Estuarine Research Reserves

Elkhorn Slough · San Francisco Bay · Tijuana River

<tr style="height:2px"><td><tr><td colspan=2 style="width:100%;padding:0px;;;" class="navbox-list navbox-even">

University of California Natural Reserve System

Año Nuevo Island · Bodega Marine · Box Springs · Boyd Deep Canyon Desert Research Center · Burns Piñon Ridge · Carpinteria Salt Marsh · Chickering American River · Coal Oil Point · Dawson Los Monos Canyon · Eagle Lake Field Station · Elliott Chaparral · Emerson Oaks · Fort Ord · Hastings · James San Jacinto Mountains · Jenny Pygmy Forest · Jepson Prairie · Kendall-Frost Mission Bay Marsh · Kenneth S. Norris Rancho Marino · Landels-Hill Big Creek · McLaughlin · Motte Rimrock · Quail Ridge · Sagehen Creek Field Station · San Joaquin Freshwater Marsh · Santa Cruz Island · Scripps Coastal · Sedgwick · Stebbins Cold Canyon · Stunt Ranch Santa Monica Mountains · Sweeney Granite Mountains Desert Research Center · Valentine Eastern Sierra · Younger Lagoon

<tr style="height:2px;"><td><tr><td class="navbox-abovebelow" style=";background:#ffc94b;" colspan="2">

Heritage registers: World Heritage Sites · World Network of Biosphere Reserves · National Register of Historic Places · National Historic Landmarks · National Natural Landmarks · California Historical Landmarks · California Points of Historical Interest · California Register of Historical Resources

Imperial National Wildlife Refuge

Imperial National Wildlife Refuge	
 Map of the United States	
Location	Imperial County, California, La Paz County, Arizona, and Yuma County, Arizona, USA
Nearest city	Yuma, Arizona
Coordinates	33°0′N 114°30′W
Area	25768 acres (104 km^2)
Established	1941
Governing body	U.S. Fish and Wildlife Service

The **Imperial National Wildlife Refuge** protects wildlife habitat along 30 miles (50 km) of the lower Colorado River in Arizona and California, including the last un-channeled section before the river enters Mexico. The **Imperial Refuge Wilderness**, a federally designated, 15056-acre (60.93 km^2), wilderness area is protected within the refuge.

The river and its associated backwater lakes and wetlands are a green oasis, contrasting with the surrounding desert mountains. It is a refuge and breeding area for migratory birds and local desert wildlife.

Wildlife

Even though it is located in the Colorado Desert and Yuma Desert, regions of the Sonoran Desert, the Imperial National Wildlife Refuge [1] is home to a mostly wetland environment. Wetland wildlife is most abundant in winter, when birds such as cinnamon teal and northern pintail use the refuge. During the summer months, permanent residents such as great egrets are abundant. The Colorado River plays a vital role in the lives of desert fauna. It is the only water source for many miles. Small animals such as the black-tailed jackrabbit and western whiptail lizard are plentiful. Desert bighorn sheep and mule deer also call the refuge home.

Birds

A full list of birds found on the refuge can be found on the refuge website.

Forest in the Desert

At one time, the banks of the Colorado River were lined with cottonwood and willow forests, sustained by the river's natural periodic flooding. Animals depended on this green forest oasis for breeding, resting, feeding, and shade. Woodcutting during the steamboat era, clearing for agriculture, wild fire, exotic plants like salt cedar, and use of dams for flood prevention have devastated cottonwood and willow stands along the lower Colorado River. Some animals that depended the riparian forests, such as the southwestern willow flycatcher (*Empidonax traillii extimus*), have become endangered.

Trails

The Painted Desert Trail is a 1.3-mile self-guided trail for an opportunity to see desert plants and wildlife. The trail takes you through a rainbow of colors left by 30,000 year-old volcanic activity and features a panoramic view of the Colorado River valley.

See also

- Colorado River
- Colorado Desert
- Yuma Desert
- Lower Colorado River Valley
- Sonny Bono Salton Sea National Wildlife Refuge

External links

- "Imperial National Wildlife Refuge" [1]. United States Fish and Wildlife Service.

<tr style="height:2px"><td><tr><td colspan=2 style="width:100%;padding:0px;;;" class="navbox-list navbox-odd">

National Forests

National Forests	Angeles · Cleveland · Eldorado · Inyo · Klamath · Lassen · Los Padres · Mendocino · Modoc · Plumas · San Bernardino · Sequoia · Shasta-Trinity · Sierra · Six Rivers · Stanislaus · Tahoe
National Wilderness Preservation System	Agua Tibia · Ansel Adams · Bucks Lake · Caribou · Carson-Iceberg · Castle Crags · Cucamonga · Desolation · Dick Smith · Dinkey Lakes · Emigrant · Golden Trout · Hoover · Inyo Mountains · Ishi · Jennie Lakes · John Muir · Kaiser · Marble Mountain · Mokelumne · Mount Shasta Wilderness · North Fork · San Gabriel · Sanhedrin · San Jacinto · San Rafael · Sespe · Siskuyou · Snow Mountain · South Fork Eel River · South Sierra · South Warner · Thousand Lakes · Trinity Alps · Ventana · Yolla Bolly-Middle Eel · Yuki
Other	Butte Valley National Grassland · Giant Sequoia National Monument · Santa Rosa and San Jacinto Mountains National Monument · Smith River National Recreation Area · Shasta-Trinity National Recreation Area

<tr style="height:2px"><td><tr><td colspan=2 style="width:100%;padding:0px;;;" class="navbox-list navbox-even">

State Forests

Boggs Mountain Demonstration · Ellen Pickett · Jackson Demonstration · Las Posadas · LaTour Demonstration · Mount Zion · Mountain Home Demonstration · Soquel Demonstration

<tr style="height:2px"><td><tr><td colspan=2 style="width:100%;padding:0px;;;" class="navbox-list navbox-odd">

National Wildlife Refuges

Antioch Dunes · Bitter Creek · Blue Ridge · Butte Sink · Castle Rock · Clear Lake · Coachella Valley · Colusa · Delevan · Don Edwards San Francisco Bay · Ellicott Slough · Farallon · Guadalupe-Nipomo Dunes · Hopper Mountain · Humboldt Bay · Kern · Lower Klamath · Marin Islands · Merced · Modoc · Pixley · Sacramento · Sacramento River · Salinas River · San Diego Bay · San Diego · San Joaquin River · San Luis · San Pablo Bay · Seal Beach · Sonny Bono Salton Sea · Stone Lakes · Sutter · Tijuana Slough · Tule Lake

<tr style="height:2px"><td><tr><td colspan=2 style="width:100%;padding:0px;;;" class="navbox-list navbox-even">

State Wildlife Areas

Wildlife AreasEcological ReservesMarine Protected Areas

Antelope Valley · Ash Creek · Bass Hill · Battle Creek · Big Lagoon · Big Sandy · Biscar · Butte Valley · Buttermilk Country · Cache Creek · Camp Cady · Cantara/Ney Springs · Cedar Roughs · Cinder Flats · Collins Eddy · Colusa Bypass · Coon Hollow · Cottonwood Creek · Crescent City Marsh · Crocker Meadows · Daugherty Hill · Decker Island · Doyle · Dutch Flat · Eastlker River · Eel

River · Elk Creek Wetlands · Elk River · Fay Slough · Feather River · Fitzhugh Creek · Fremont Weir · Grass Lake · Gray Lodge · Green Creek · Grizzly Island · Hallelujah Junction · Heenan Lake · Hill Slough · Hollenbeck Canyon · Honey Lake · Hope Valley · Horseshoe Ranch · Imperial · Indian Valley · Kelso Peak and Old Dad Mountains · Kinsman Flat · Knoxville · Laguna · Lake Berryessa · Lake Earl · Lake Sonoma · Little Panoche Reservoir · Los Banos · Lower Sherman Island · Mad River Slough · Marble Mountains · Mendota · Merrill's Landing · Miner Slough · Monache Meadows · Morro Bay · Moss Landing · Mouth of Cottonwood Creek · Napa-Sonoma Marshes · North Grasslands · O'Neill Forebay · Oroville · Petaluma Marsh · Pickel Meadow · Pine Creek · Point Edith · Putah Creek · Rector Reservoir · Red Lake · Rhode Island · Sacramento River · San Felipe Valley · San Jacinto · San Luis Obispo · San Luis Reservoir · San Pablo Bay · Santa Rosa · Shasta Valley · Silver Creek · Slinkard/Little Antelope · Smithneck Creek · South Fork · Spenceville · Surprise Valley · Sutter Bypass · Tehama · Truckee River · Upper Butte Basin · Volta · Warner Valley · Waukell Creek · West Hilmar · Westlker River · White Slough · Willow Creek · Yolo Bypass

Albany Mudflats · Alkali Sink · Allensworth · Atascadero Creek Marsh · Bair Island · Baldwin Lake · Batiquitos Lagoon · Blue Sky · Boden Canyon · Boggs Lake · Bolsa Chica · Bonny Doon · Buena Vista Lagoon · Butler Slough · Butte Creek Canyon · Butte Creek House · Buttonwillow · By Day Creek · Calhoun Cut · Canebrake · Carlsbad Highlands · Carmel Bay · Carrizo Canyon · Carrizo Plains · China Point · Clover Creek · Coachella Valley · Coal Canyon · Corte Madera Marsh · Crestridge · Dairy Mart Ponds · Dales Lake · Del Mar Landing · Elkhorn Slough · Estelle Mountain · Fall River Mills · Fish Slough · Fremont Valley · Goleta Slough · Indian Joe Spring · Kaweah · Kerman · King Clone · Laguna Laurel · Loch Lomond Vernal Pool · Lokern · Magnesia Spring · Marin Islands · Mattole River · McGinty Mountain · Morro Dunes · Morro Rock · Napa River · North Table Mountain · Oasis Spring · Panoche Hills · Peytonia Slough · Pine Hill · Piute Creek · Pleasant Valley · Point Lobos · Rancho Jamul · Redwood Shores · River Springs Lakes · Saline Valley · San Dieguito Lagoon · San Elijo Lagoon · San Felipe Creek · San Joaquin River · Santa Rosa Plateau · Springville · Stone Corral · Sycamore Canyon · Sycuan Peak · Thomes Creek · Tomales Bay · Upper Newport Bay · Watsonville Slough · West Mojave Desert · Woodbridge · Yaudanchi

Abalone Cove · Agua Hedionda Lagoon · Albany Mudflats · Anacapa · Anacapa · Año Nuevo · Asilomar · Atascadero Beach · Bair Island · Batiquitos Lagoon · Big Creek · Big Creek · Big Sycamore Canyon · Bodega · Bolsa Chica · Buena Vista Lagoon · Cambria · Cardiff and San Elijo · Carmel Bay · Carmel Pinnacles · Carrington Point · Catalina Marine Science Center · Corte Madera Marsh · Crystal Cove · Dana Point · Del Mar Landing · Doheny · Doheny · Duxbury Reef · Edward F. Ricketts · Elkhorn Slough · Elkhorn Slough · Encinitas · Estero de Limantour · Fagan Marsh · Farallon Islands · Farnsworth Bank · Fort Ross · Gerstle Cove · Goleta Slough · Greyhound Rock · Gull Island · Harris Point · Heisler Park · Hopkins · Irvine Coast · James V. Fitzgerald · Judith Rock · Julia Pfeiffer Burns · La Jolla · Laguna Beach · Lovers Cove (Catalina Island) · Lovers Point · MacKerricher · Manchester and Arena Rock · Marin Islands · Mia J. Tegner · Moro Cojo Slough · Morro Bay · Morro Bay · Morro Beach · Natural Bridges · Niguel · Pacific Grove Marine Gardens · Painted Cave · Peytonia Slough ·

Piedras Blancas · Piedras Blancas · Pismo · Pismo-Oceano Beach · Point Buchon · Point Buchon · Point Cabrillo · Point Fermin · Point Lobos · Point Reyes Headlands · Point Sur · Point Sur · Portuguese Ledge · Punta Gorda · Redwood Shores · Refugio · Richardson Rock · Robert E. Badham · Robert W. Crown · Russian Gulch · Russian River · Salt Point · San Diego-Scripps · San Dieguito Lagoon · San Elijo Lagoon · Santa Barbara Island · Scorpion · Skunk Point · Sonoma Coast · Soquel Canyon · South Laguna Beach · South Point · Tomales Bay · Upper Newport Bay · Van Damme · Vandenberg · White Rock (Cambria)

<tr style="height:2px"><td><tr><td colspan=2 style="width:100%;padding:0px;;;" class="navbox-list navbox-odd">

National Landscape Conservation System

National Monuments	California Coastal · Carrizo Plain · Santa Rosa and San Jacinto Mountains
National Conservation Areas	California Desert · King Range
Wilderness Areas	Argus Range · Big Maria Mountains · Bigelow Cholla Garden · Bighorn Mountain · Black Mountain · Bright Star · Bristol Mountains · Cadiz Dunes · Carrizo Gorge · Chemehuevi Mountains · Chimney Peak · Chuckwalla Mountains · Chumash · Cleghorn Lakes · Clipper Mountain · Coso Range · Coyote Mountains · Darwin Falls · Dead Mountains · Dick Smith · El Paso Mountains · Fish Creek Mountains · Funeral Mountains · Golden Valley · Grass Valley · Headwaters Forest Reserve · Hollow Hills · Ibex · Indian Pass · Inyo Mountains · Jacumba · Kelso Dunes · Kiavah · Kingston Range · Little Chuckwalla Mountains · Little Picacho · Machesna Mountain · Matilija · Malpais Mesa · Manly Peak · Mecca Hills · Mesquite · Newberry Mountains · Nopah Range · North Algodones Dunes · North Mesquite Mountains · Old Woman Mountains · Orocopia Mountains · Otay Mountain · Owens Peak · Pahrump Valley · Palen/McCoy · Palo Verde Mountains · Picacho Peak · Piper Mountain · Piute Mountains · Red Buttes · Resting Spring Range · Rice Valley · Riverside Mountains · Rodman Mountains · Sacatar Trail · Saddle Peak Hills · San Gorgonio · Santa Lucia · Santa Rosa · Sawtooth Mountains · Sespe · Sheephole Valley · South Nopah Range · Stateline · Stepladder Mountains · Surprise Canyon · Sylvania Mountains · Trilobite · Turtle Mountains · Whipple Mountains ·

<tr style="height:2px"><td><tr><td colspan=2 style="width:100%;padding:0px;;;" class="navbox-list navbox-even">

National Marine Sanctuaries

Channel Islands · Cordell Bank · Gulf of the Farallones · Monterey Bay

```
<tr style="height:2px"><td><tr><td colspan=2 style="width:100%;padding:0px;;;" class="navbox-list
navbox-odd">
```

National Estuarine Research Reserves

Elkhorn Slough · San Francisco Bay · Tijuana River

```
<tr style="height:2px"><td><tr><td colspan=2 style="width:100%;padding:0px;;;" class="navbox-list
navbox-even">
```

University of California Natural Reserve System

Año Nuevo Island · Bodega Marine · Box Springs · Boyd Deep Canyon Desert Research Center · Burns Piñon Ridge · Carpinteria Salt Marsh · Chickering American River · Coal Oil Point · Dawson Los Monos Canyon · Eagle Lake Field Station · Elliott Chaparral · Emerson Oaks · Fort Ord · Hastings · James San Jacinto Mountains · Jenny Pygmy Forest · Jepson Prairie · Kendall-Frost Mission Bay Marsh · Kenneth S. Norris Rancho Marino · Landels-Hill Big Creek · McLaughlin · Motte Rimrock · Quail Ridge · Sagehen Creek Field Station · San Joaquin Freshwater Marsh · Santa Cruz Island · Scripps Coastal · Sedgwick · Stebbins Cold Canyon · Stunt Ranch Santa Monica Mountains · Sweeney Granite Mountains Desert Research Center · Valentine Eastern Sierra · Younger Lagoon

```
<tr     style="height:2px;"><td><tr><td     class="navbox-abovebelow"     style=";background:#ffc94b;"
colspan="2">
```

Heritage registers: World Heritage Sites · World Network of Biosphere Reserves · National Register of Historic Places · National Historic Landmarks · National Natural Landmarks · California Historical Landmarks · California Points of Historical Interest · California Register of Historical Resources

Sonny Bono Salton Sea National Wildlife Refuge

Sonny Bono Salton Sea National Wildlife Refuge	
Map of the United States	
Location	Imperial County, California, USA
Nearest city	Brawley, California
Coordinates	33°9′N 115°44′W
Area	2200 acres (9 km^2)
Established	1930
Governing body	U.S. Fish and Wildlife Service

The **Sonny Bono Salton Sea National Wildlife Refuge** is located 40 miles (64 km) north of the Mexican border at the southern end of the Salton Sea in California's Imperial Valley. Situated along the Pacific Flyway, the Refuge is the only one of its kind, located 227 feet (69 m) below sea level. Because of its southern latitude, elevation and location in the Colorado Desert, the Refuge experiences some of the highest temperatures in the nation. Daily temperatures from May to October generally exceed 100°F with temperatures of 116°–120°F recorded yearly.

History

The refuge was established as a sanctuary and breeding ground for birds and wild animals in 1930. In 1998, the refuge was renamed after Congressman Sonny Bono, who played an active role in trying to save the Salton Sea. Originally, it included approximately 37600 acres (15200 ha). Nearly 60 percent of the original acreage was an open saline lake with the remainder being shoreline alkali flats, freshwater wetlands, native desert scrub and upland (farm fields). Due to the inflow of agricultural effluent and a subsequent rise in the level of the Salton Sea, all of the original Refuge area has been inundated. At present, only about 2,200 manageable acres remain suitable for farming and wetland development.

Geography

The topography of the Sonny Bono Salton Sea NWR is flat, except for Rock Hill, which is located at the refuge headquarters. The refuge is bordered by the Salton Sea on the north and intensively farmed agricultural lands on the east, south and west.

The refuge is composed of two disjunctive units, separated by 18 miles (29 km) of private lands. Each unit contains managed wetland habitat, agricultural fields, and tree rows. The courses of the New and Alamo rivers run through the refuge, providing freshwater inflow to the Salton Sea.

Refuge habitats

The Sonny Bono Salton Sea National Wildlife Refuge was established in 1930 by executive order as a breeding ground for birds and wild animals. Primary objectives on the refuge include endangered species production and maintenance, sensitive species production and maintenance, wintering waterfowl maintenance, and other migratory bird management. Refuge habitats are intensively managed. Ponds, forests, and agricultural fields are designed, developed and manipulated to achieve wildlife objectives.

Wetlands

The refuge has 826 acres (334 ha) of manageable wetland units, which are managed for resident and migratory bird species such as waterfowl, shorebirds and wading birds. In addition, specified impoundments are managed as permanent wetlands to provide critical nesting and year-round habitat for the endangered Yuma clapper rail. Refuge wetlands provide nesting habitat for a variety of other species, including the least bittern, white-faced ibis, black-necked stilt and American avocet. All wetlands are flooded from water supplied by the Imperial Irrigation District. This water is termed "class 1" irrigation water, which is free of fertilizers, toxic pesticides and high levels of salts that are common in agricultural drain water.

Tree rows

The refuge manages tree rows for native species and biodiversity. Species planted include honey mesquite, screwbean mesquite, blue palo verde, Mexican palo verde, fairy duster, sweet acacia, catclaw acacia, and desert ironwood. Tree rows continue to receive additional plantings throughout the year in order to add density and width, and to better meet wildlife and habitat objectives.

Croplands

Wildlife management at the Sonny Bono Salton Sea NWR involves an intensive farming program to provide suitable forage for over 30,000 wintering geese and other migratory birds and wildlife. Croplands comprise of 869 acres (352 ha) on the refuge, with many fields cooperatively farmed by local farmers.

Crops planted on refuge land includes alfalfa, wheat, rye grass, milo, millet, and sudan grass. With use restrictions on the use of certain pesticides on the refuge, infestations of white flies, and the booming prices of sudan grass, many cooperative farmers have switched from planting alfalfa to sudan grass over the years. Sudan grass grows like a weed in the Imperial Valley and requires little to no use of pesticides.

Wildlife

The Sonny Bono Salton Sea NWR is geographically located within the southwestern edge of the Colorado zone of the Sonoran Desert biome. This location, coupled with an elevation of 227 feet (69 m) below sea level, results in extremely low annual precipitation and extremely high day time temperatures. Despite the harsh environmental conditions, the Salton Sea supports one of the most diverse avian compositions in the United States as well as a host of endangered and other wildlife species.

Habitat diversity on Refuge lands provides for the needs of resident wildlife species as well as numerous seasonal residents and migrants of the Pacific Flyway. Over 400 bird species have been recorded at the Refuge and at least 93 species have nested on the Refuge. In addition, 41 species of mammals, 18 species of reptiles, 4 species of amphibians and 15 species of fish have been identified in the area.

Numbers and species of birds that can be seen on the Refuge vary according to season. Heavy migrations of waterfowl, marsh and shorebirds occur during spring and fall. Throughout the mild winter and spring a wide variety of songbirds and birds of prey are present. They are attracted to the freshwater marshes and riparian habitat along the New and Alamo rivers. The greatest number of species are present from November to May.

Mammals

Visibility varies greatly from species to species due to the nocturnal habits of some and seasonal hibernation of others. Most rodent species exist in terrestrial habitats where they provide important food resources for raptors and other predators. During winter months, rodents provide food for heron and egret species as well. Muskrats are present in freshwater drains and ponds where their feeding and burrowing activities help maintain marsh habitats for various other wildlife species.

- Desert Cottontail

- Merriam's kangaroo rat
- Raccoon
- Valley pocket gopher
- Coyote
- Round-tailed ground squirrel
- Striped skunk
- Desert pocket mouse
- Muskrat

Amphibians

Due to environmental factors, amphibians are not found in large numbers or diversity at the Sonny Bono Salton Sea NWR. Species occurring on the refuge include bullfrogs and lowland leopard frogs. Lowland leopard frogs respond well to shallow, permanent wetland habitat created for the Yuma clapper rail. They are not present elsewhere on the Refuge due to competition from exotic bullfrogs. Woodhouse's toad and red-spotted toads are also found on the refuge.

Reptiles

Many different species of reptiles occur on the refuge. Common species include the gopher snake, western diamondback snake, coachwhip, common kingsnake, whiptail lizard, desert spiny lizard and side-blotched lizard. The spiny soft-shell turtle and the desert tortoise are also found on the refuge. Spiny soft-shell turtles are found in freshwater drains and ponds, while the desert tortoise, although rarely seen, can be found in the upland desert areas.

Fish

Fish populations thrive in the Salton Sea. The aquatic ecosystem is extremely productive because of the large amounts of nutrients it receives. The nutrients stimulate growth of phytoplankton and algae, which in turn, support zooplankton and worms. All of this provides a continuing supply of food for fish. Periodically, decomposition of large algal blooms diminishes the dissolved oxygen in the water. This decomposition has been tied to occasional fish die-offs that occur throughout the year.

Tilapia is the most common fish found in the Salton Sea. Tilapia is the most populous fish in the Sea due to its ability to adapt to highly saline conditions and the fact that it is a prolific breeder. Tilapia are an important food source for birds and other fish, along with being a popular game fish. They can weigh more than 3 pounds (1.4 kg).

Endangered Species

- California Brown Pelican
- Yuma Clapper Rail
- Desert pupfish

Trails

The refuge has two walking trails: the Rock Hill Trail and the Michael Hardenberger Trail. The Rock Hill Trail is approximately 2 miles (3.2 km) roundtrip, leading visitors through several different habitats. It begins next to the picnic area at the Visitor Center and ends on the top of Rock Hill (33°11′0″N 115°37′23″W), which is located on the edge of the Salton Sea.

The Michael Hardenberger Trail is located at Unit 1 off Vendel Road, which is at the south end of the Salton Sea. The ½-mile trail encircles one of the freshwater ponds, a favorite nesting spot for the endangered Yuma clapper rail.

External links

- Sonny Bono Salton Sea National Wildlife Refuge website [1]
- Bird Checklist for the Salton Sea National Wildlife Refuge [2]
- Mammal Checklists [3]
- Amphibian and Reptile Checklists [4]
- Fish Checklists [5]

See also

- Salton Sea State Recreation Area
- Colorado Desert
- Salton Sea
- Salton Sink
- Coachella Valley
- Imperial National Wildlife Refuge

- Protected areas of the Colorado Desert
- Wilderness Areas within the Lower Colorado River Valley

References

<tr style="height:2px"><td><tr><td colspan=2 style="width:100%;padding:0px;;;" class="navbox-list navbox-odd">

National Forests

National Forests	Angeles · Cleveland · Eldorado · Inyo · Klamath · Lassen · Los Padres · Mendocino · Modoc · Plumas · San Bernardino · Sequoia · Shasta-Trinity · Sierra · Six Rivers · Stanislaus · Tahoe
National Wilderness Preservation System	Agua Tibia · Ansel Adams · Bucks Lake · Caribou · Carson-Iceberg · Castle Crags · Cucamonga · Desolation · Dick Smith · Dinkey Lakes · Emigrant · Golden Trout · Hoover · Inyo Mountains · Ishi · Jennie Lakes · John Muir · Kaiser · Marble Mountain · Mokelumne · Mount Shasta Wilderness · North Fork · San Gabriel · Sanhedrin · San Jacinto · San Rafael · Sespe · Siskuyou · Snow Mountain · South Fork Eel River · South Sierra · South Warner · Thousand Lakes · Trinity Alps · Ventana · Yolla Bolly-Middle Eel · Yuki
Other	Butte Valley National Grassland · Giant Sequoia National Monument · Santa Rosa and San Jacinto Mountains National Monument · Smith River National Recreation Area · Shasta-Trinity National Recreation Area

<tr style="height:2px"><td><tr><td colspan=2 style="width:100%;padding:0px;;;" class="navbox-list navbox-even">

State Forests

Boggs Mountain Demonstration · Ellen Pickett · Jackson Demonstration · Las Posadas · LaTour Demonstration · Mount Zion · Mountain Home Demonstration · Soquel Demonstration

<tr style="height:2px"><td><tr><td colspan=2 style="width:100%;padding:0px;;;" class="navbox-list navbox-odd">

National Wildlife Refuges

Antioch Dunes · Bitter Creek · Blue Ridge · Butte Sink · Castle Rock · Clear Lake · Coachella Valley · Colusa · Delevan · Don Edwards San Francisco Bay · Ellicott Slough · Farallon · Guadalupe-Nipomo Dunes · Hopper Mountain · Humboldt Bay · Kern · Lower Klamath · Marin Islands · Merced · Modoc · Pixley · Sacramento · Sacramento River · Salinas River · San Diego Bay · San Diego · San Joaquin River · San Luis · San Pablo Bay · Seal Beach · Sonny Bono Salton Sea · Stone Lakes · Sutter · Tijuana Slough · Tule Lake

<tr style="height:2px"><td><tr><td colspan=2 style="width:100%;padding:0px;;;" class="navbox-list navbox-even">

State Wildlife Areas

Wildlife AreasEcological ReservesMarine Protected Areas

Antelope Valley · Ash Creek · Bass Hill · Battle Creek · Big Lagoon · Big Sandy · Biscar · Butte Valley · Buttermilk Country · Cache Creek · Camp Cady · Cantara/Ney Springs · Cedar Roughs · Cinder Flats · Collins Eddy · Colusa Bypass · Coon Hollow · Cottonwood Creek · Crescent City Marsh · Crocker Meadows · Daugherty Hill · Decker Island · Doyle · Dutch Flat · Eastlker River · Eel River · Elk Creek Wetlands · Elk River · Fay Slough · Feather River · Fitzhugh Creek · Fremont Weir · Grass Lake · Gray Lodge · Green Creek · Grizzly Island · Hallelujah Junction · Heenan Lake · Hill Slough · Hollenbeck Canyon · Honey Lake · Hope Valley · Horseshoe Ranch · Imperial · Indian Valley · Kelso Peak and Old Dad Mountains · Kinsman Flat · Knoxville · Laguna · Lake Berryessa · Lake Earl · Lake Sonoma · Little Panoche Reservoir · Los Banos · Lower Sherman Island · Mad River Slough · Marble Mountains · Mendota · Merrill's Landing · Miner Slough · Monache Meadows · Morro Bay · Moss Landing · Mouth of Cottonwood Creek · Napa-Sonoma Marshes · North Grasslands · O'Neill Forebay · Oroville · Petaluma Marsh · Pickel Meadow · Pine Creek · Point Edith · Putah Creek · Rector Reservoir · Red Lake · Rhode Island · Sacramento River · San Felipe Valley · San Jacinto · San Luis Obispo · San Luis Reservoir · San Pablo Bay · Santa Rosa · Shasta Valley · Silver Creek · Slinkard/Little Antelope · Smithneck Creek · South Fork · Spenceville · Surprise Valley · Sutter Bypass · Tehama · Truckee River · Upper Butte Basin · Volta · Warner Valley · Waukell Creek · West Hilmar · Westlker River · White Slough · Willow Creek · Yolo Bypass

Albany Mudflats · Alkali Sink · Allensworth · Atascadero Creek Marsh · Bair Island · Baldwin Lake · Batiquitos Lagoon · Blue Sky · Boden Canyon · Boggs Lake · Bolsa Chica · Bonny Doon · Buena Vista Lagoon · Butler Slough · Butte Creek Canyon · Butte Creek House · Buttonwillow · By Day Creek · Calhoun Cut · Canebrake · Carlsbad Highlands · Carmel Bay · Carrizo Canyon · Carrizo Plains · China Point · Clover Creek · Coachella Valley · Coal Canyon · Corte Madera Marsh · Crestridge · Dairy Mart Ponds · Dales Lake · Del Mar Landing · Elkhorn Slough · Estelle Mountain · Fall River Mills · Fish Slough · Fremont Valley · Goleta Slough · Indian Joe Spring · Kaweah · Kerman · King Clone · Laguna Laurel · Loch Lomond Vernal Pool · Lokern · Magnesia Spring · Marin Islands · Mattole River · McGinty Mountain · Morro Dunes · Morro Rock · Napa River · North Table Mountain · Oasis Spring · Panoche Hills · Peytonia Slough · Pine Hill · Piute Creek · Pleasant Valley · Point Lobos · Rancho Jamul · Redwood Shores · River Springs Lakes · Saline Valley · San Dieguito Lagoon · San Elijo Lagoon · San Felipe Creek · San Joaquin River · Santa Rosa Plateau · Springville · Stone Corral · Sycamore Canyon · Sycuan Peak · Thomes Creek · Tomales Bay · Upper Newport Bay · Watsonville Slough · West Mojave Desert · Woodbridge · Yaudanchi

Abalone Cove · Agua Hedionda Lagoon · Albany Mudflats · Anacapa · Anacapa · Año Nuevo · Asilomar · Atascadero Beach · Bair Island · Batiquitos Lagoon · Big Creek · Big Creek · Big Sycamore Canyon · Bodega · Bolsa Chica · Buena Vista Lagoon · Cambria · Cardiff and San Elijo · Carmel Bay · Carmel Pinnacles · Carrington Point · Catalina Marine Science Center · Corte Madera Marsh · Crystal Cove · Dana Point · Del Mar Landing · Doheny · Doheny · Duxbury Reef · Edward F. Ricketts · Elkhorn Slough · Elkhorn Slough · Encinitas · Estero de Limantour · Fagan Marsh · Farallon Islands · Farnsworth Bank · Fort Ross · Gerstle Cove · Goleta Slough · Greyhound Rock · Gull Island · Harris

Point · Heisler Park · Hopkins · Irvine Coast · James V. Fitzgerald · Judith Rock · Julia Pfeiffer Burns · La Jolla · Laguna Beach · Lovers Cove (Catalina Island) · Lovers Point · MacKerricher · Manchester and Arena Rock · Marin Islands · Mia J. Tegner · Moro Cojo Slough · Morro Bay · Morro Bay · Morro Beach · Natural Bridges · Niguel · Pacific Grove Marine Gardens · Painted Cave · Peytonia Slough · Piedras Blancas · Piedras Blancas · Pismo · Pismo-Oceano Beach · Point Buchon · Point Buchon · Point Cabrillo · Point Fermin · Point Lobos · Point Reyes Headlands · Point Sur · Point Sur · Portuguese Ledge · Punta Gorda · Redwood Shores · Refugio · Richardson Rock · Robert E. Badham · Robert W. Crown · Russian Gulch · Russian River · Salt Point · San Diego-Scripps · San Dieguito Lagoon · San Elijo Lagoon · Santa Barbara Island · Scorpion · Skunk Point · Sonoma Coast · Soquel Canyon · South Laguna Beach · South Point · Tomales Bay · Upper Newport Bay · Van Damme · Vandenberg · White Rock (Cambria)

```
<tr style="height:2px"><td><tr><td colspan=2 style="width:100%;padding:0px;;;" class="navbox-list
navbox-odd">
```

National Landscape Conservation System

National Monuments	California Coastal · Carrizo Plain · Santa Rosa and San Jacinto Mountains
National Conservation Areas	California Desert · King Range
Wilderness Areas	Argus Range · Big Maria Mountains · Bigelow Cholla Garden · Bighorn Mountain · Black Mountain · Bright Star · Bristol Mountains · Cadiz Dunes · Carrizo Gorge · Chemehuevi Mountains · Chimney Peak · Chuckwalla Mountains · Chumash · Cleghorn Lakes · Clipper Mountain · Coso Range · Coyote Mountains · Darwin Falls · Dead Mountains · Dick Smith · El Paso Mountains · Fish Creek Mountains · Funeral Mountains · Golden Valley · Grass Valley · Headwaters Forest Reserve · Hollow Hills · Ibex · Indian Pass · Inyo Mountains · Jacumba · Kelso Dunes · Kiavah · Kingston Range · Little Chuckwalla Mountains · Little Picacho · Machesna Mountain · Matilija · Malpais Mesa · Manly Peak · Mecca Hills · Mesquite · Newberry Mountains · Nopah Range · North Algodones Dunes · North Mesquite Mountains · Old Woman Mountains · Orocopia Mountains · Otay Mountain · Owens Peak · Pahrump Valley · Palen/McCoy · Palo Verde Mountains · Picacho Peak · Piper Mountain · Piute Mountains · Red Buttes · Resting Spring Range · Rice Valley · Riverside Mountains · Rodman Mountains · Sacatar Trail · Saddle Peak Hills · San Gorgonio · Santa Lucia · Santa Rosa · Sawtooth Mountains · Sespe · Sheephole Valley · South Nopah Range · Stateline · Stepladder Mountains · Surprise Canyon · Sylvania Mountains · Trilobite · Turtle Mountains · Whipple Mountains ·

```
<tr style="height:2px"><td><tr><td colspan=2 style="width:100%;padding:0px;;;" class="navbox-list
navbox-even">
```

National Marine Sanctuaries

Channel Islands · Cordell Bank · Gulf of the Farallones · Monterey Bay

<tr style="height:2px"><td><tr><td colspan=2 style="width:100%;padding:0px;;;" class="navbox-list navbox-odd">

National Estuarine Research Reserves

Elkhorn Slough · San Francisco Bay · Tijuana River

<tr style="height:2px"><td><tr><td colspan=2 style="width:100%;padding:0px;;;" class="navbox-list navbox-even">

University of California Natural Reserve System

Año Nuevo Island · Bodega Marine · Box Springs · Boyd Deep Canyon Desert Research Center · Burns Piñon Ridge · Carpinteria Salt Marsh · Chickering American River · Coal Oil Point · Dawson Los Monos Canyon · Eagle Lake Field Station · Elliott Chaparral · Emerson Oaks · Fort Ord · Hastings · James San Jacinto Mountains · Jenny Pygmy Forest · Jepson Prairie · Kendall-Frost Mission Bay Marsh · Kenneth S. Norris Rancho Marino · Landels-Hill Big Creek · McLaughlin · Motte Rimrock · Quail Ridge · Sagehen Creek Field Station · San Joaquin Freshwater Marsh · Santa Cruz Island · Scripps Coastal · Sedgwick · Stebbins Cold Canyon · Stunt Ranch Santa Monica Mountains · Sweeney Granite Mountains Desert Research Center · Valentine Eastern Sierra · Younger Lagoon

<tr style="height:2px;"><td><tr><td class="navbox-abovebelow" style=";background:#ffc94b;" colspan="2">

Heritage registers: World Heritage Sites · World Network of Biosphere Reserves · National Register of Historic Places · National Historic Landmarks · National Natural Landmarks · California Historical Landmarks · California Points of Historical Interest · California Register of Historical Resources

]

Cibola National Wildlife Refuge

Cibola National Wildlife Refuge is located in the floodplain of the lower Colorado River between Arizona and California and surrounded by a fringe of desert ridges and washes. The refuge encompasses both the historic Colorado River channel as well as a channelized portion constructed in the late 1960s. Along with these main waterbodies, several important backwaters are home to many wildlife species that reside in this Yuma Desert portion of the Sonoran Desert. Because of the river's life sustaining water, wildlife here survive in an environment that reaches 120 degrees in the summer and receives an average of only 2 inches of rain per year.

Importance

The Refuge is one of the last major stop overs of the Pacific Flyway for migratory birds. Over 250 species of birds have been identified at Cibola NWR, including Canada Geese, Sandhill Cranes, Snowy Egrets, and the endangered Southwestern Willow Flycatcher. Other species that inhabit the area include; Mule Deer, Gamble's Quail, Bobcat, Golden Eagles, and Coyotes.

Operations

Cibola NWR undertakes major projects annually including the conservation of a desert pupfish population, one of three that exist in Arizona. Invasive species removal of many detrimental species enhances natural riparian habitat, and provides hunting opportunities for the public. In return, populations are regulated and the sustainability of the ecosystem is maintained.

References

- Refuge profile [1]
- Refuge website [2]

@ *This article incorporates public domain material from websites or documents of the United States Fish and Wildlife Service.*

Geographical coordinates: 33°18′42″N 114°41′21″W

Yuma Crossing

Yuma Crossing and Associated Sites	
U.S. National Register of Historic Places	
U.S. National Historic Landmark	
Nearest city:	Winterhaven, California and Yuma, Arizona
Coordinates:	32°43′43″N 114°36′56″W
Built/Founded:	1852
Governing body:	State
Added to NRHP:	November 13, 1966
Designated NHL:	November 13, 1966
NRHP Reference#:	66000197

Yuma Crossing is a site in Arizona and California that is significant for its association with transportation and communication across the Colorado River. It connected New Spain and Las Californias in the Spanish Colonial period in and also during the Western expansion of the United States. Features of the Arizona side include the Yuma Quartermaster Depot and Yuma Territorial Prison. Features on the California Side include Fort Yuma which protected the area from 1850 to 1885

History

The history of the Yuma Crossing began at the formation of two massive granite outcroppings on the Colorado River. The narrowing of the river provided the only crossing point for a thousand miles, thus making it a focal point for the Patayan tribes, and later the Quechan.

In 1540, before the British Europeans touched Plymouth Rock in 1620, Yuma's European history began here with the arrival of Spanish explorer Hernando de Alarcon. Much later the Yuma Crossing became the focal point for travel to the Wild West, from the 1840s California Gold Rush era to the arrival of the railroad in the 1870s, and finally the Ocean-to-Ocean Bridge, which linked the East coast and the West coast in one land route.

It was declared a National Historic Landmark in 1966, under the name **Yuma Crossing and Associated Sites**.

National Heritage Area

The **Yuma Crossing National Heritage Area**, located at Yuma Crossing, is a U.S. National Heritage Area. It was the only lower Colorado River crossing point in the 18th and 19th centuries for non-Native American travelers and immigrants. The Heritage Area is part of the Yuma Crossing and Associated Sites on the National Register of Historic Places and a National Historic Landmark, in Arizona and California.

As with other U.S. National Heritage Areas, the Yuma Crossing National Heritage Area is a local entity in partnership with various stakeholders. At Yuma Crossing, the stakeholders are particularly diverse, including Indian tribes, agricultural interests, environmental and wildlife non-profit organizations, as well as many federal, states, and local agencies.

History park

The Yuma Crossing National Heritage Area includes the Yuma Quartermaster Depot State Historic Park (*formerly known as Yuma Crossing State Historic Park*), the Yuma Territorial Prison, Fort Yuma, and other sites, all showcasing the area's history. They are amidst the beautiful and vital Yuma East and West Wetlands, and against the silhouetted backdrops of the Castle Dome, Chocolate (Arizona) and Chocolate (California) Mountains.

The heritage area's interpretive themes include Yuma's importance as a cultural crossroads, emphasizing the region's intersection of three major cultures: Anglo-American, Native American, and Hispanic-Latino. The heritage area recognizes that this rich blend of traditions can best be sustained by their continued expression through architecture, art, music, food, and folkways within the heritage area.

Juan Bautista de Anza National Historic Trail

The Yuma Crossing is one of the designated tour sights of the Juan Bautista de Anza National Historic Trail, a National Park Service unit in the United States National Historic Trail and National Millennium Trail programs. A Brochure Map for driving [1] and detailed Maps by County [2], with a Historical destinations-events Guide [3] and the official NPS: Juan Bautista de Anza National Historic Trail website [14] are all available for information about the historic 1776 Juan Bautista de Anza trail places.

Habitat restoration

The Yuma Heritage Area has championed a wetland and riparian habitat restoration project for the East Wetlands, including returning the Colorado's water flow, in a multiyear, multimillion-dollar effort. In 2004, heritage area partners secured a Clean Water Act permit from the U.S. Army Corps of Engineers to begin restoration work. More than 200 acres (0.81 km^2) of nonnative invasive species vegetation have been removed and more than 130 acres (0.53 km^2) have been replanted with cottonwoods, willow, mesquite, native bunchgrasses, and palo verde trees. A one-mile (1.6 km) length of back channel has also been excavated, and some 20,000 new trees were planted in 2006.

To date, ten different funding sources have provided almost $6 million toward the eventual goal of $18–20 million to complete the project. The current executive director of the heritage area is Charles W. Flynn.

Area plant life

- Fremont cottonwood - *Populus fremontii*
- Catclaw Acacia - *Acacia greggii*
- Blue Palo Verde - *Parkinsonia florida*
- Velvet mesquite - *Prosopis velutina*
- Screwbean Mesquite - *Prosopis pubescens* - "Tornillo"
- Honey Mesquite - *Prosopis glandulosa*
- Goodding's black willow - *Salix gooddingii*
- Arroyo Willow - *Salix lasiolepis*

See also

- Quechan
- Spanish period of Arizona
- Mexican period of Arizona
- Territorial evolution of California
- Alta California
- History of California to 1899
- Mesquite Bosque

External links

- Yuma Quartermaster Depot [4]
- Yume Territorial Prison [5]
- Fort Yuma history [6]
- official U.S. National Park Service Juan Bautista de Anza National Historic Trail website [14]
- official **Yuma Crossing National Heritage Area** website [7]

Transportation

Imperial County Airport

Imperial County Airport Boley Field	
IATA: IPL – ICAO: KIPL – FAA LID: IPL	
Summary	
Airport type	Public
Operator	Imperial County
Location	Imperial, California
Hub for	{{{hub}}}
Elevation AMSL	-56 ft / -17.1 m
Coordinates	32°50′03″N 115°34′43″W

Runways			
Direction	Length		Surface
	ft	m	
14/32	5,304	1,617	Asphalt
8/26	4,500	1,372	Asphalt

Imperial County Airport (IATA: **IPL**, ICAO: **KIPL**, FAA LID: **IPL**), also known as **Boley Field,** is a public airport located partially in the city of Imperial and partially in an unincorporated area in Imperial County, California, United States. The airport is located 0.94 miles (1.5 km) south of the central business district (CBD) of Imperial. The airport serves nearby communities, including El Centro. The airport covers 429 acres (174 ha) and has two runways. It is mostly used for general aviation, but is served by one commercial airline. Service is subsidized by the Essential Air Service program.

Airline

Airlines	Destinations
United Express operated by SkyWest Airlines	Los Angeles, Yuma

References

- FAA Airport Master Record for IPL [1] (Form 5010 [2] PDF)

External links

- [3] (Imperial County Airport web site, includes airport information)
- Resources for this airport:
    - AirNav airport information for KIPL [4]
    - ASN accident history for IPL [5]
    - FlightAware airport information [6] and live flight tracker [7]
    - NOAA/NWS latest weather observations [8]
    - SkyVector aeronautical chart [9], Terminal Procedures [10] for KIPL

Calexico International Airport

Calexico International Airport	
IATA: CXL – ICAO: KCXL – FAA LID: CXL	
Summary	
Airport type	Public
Owner	City of Calexico
Serves	Calexico, California
Hub for	{{{hub}}}
Elevation AMSL	4 ft / 1 m
Coordinates	Geographical coordinates: 32°40′10″N 115°30′48″W

Runways			
Direction	Length		Surface
	ft	m	
8/26	4,679	1,426	Asphalt

Statistics (2004)	
Aircraft operations	12,240
Based aircraft	23

Source: Federal Aviation Administration

Calexico International Airport (IATA: **CXL**, ICAO: **KCXL**, FAA LID: **CXL**) is a city-owned public-use airport located one mile (1.6 km) west of the central business district of Calexico, in Imperial County, California, United States. The airport is mostly used for general aviation and to facilitate border crossing.

Facilities and aircraft

Calexico International Airport covers an area of 257 acres (104 ha) which contains one asphalt paved runway (8/26) measuring 4,679 x 75 ft (1,426 x 23 m). For the 12-month period ending December 31, 2004, the airport had 12,240 aircraft operations, an average of 33 per day: 93% general aviation and 7% air taxi. At that time there were 23 aircraft based at this airport: 83% single-engine and 17% multi-engine.

External links

- Calexico International Airport [1] page at City of Calexico website
- Resources for this airport:
    - AirNav airport information for CXL [2]
    - ASN accident history for CXL [3]
    - FlightAware airport information [4] and live flight tracker [5]
    - SkyVector aeronautical chart for CXL [6]

Imperial Valley Transit

Parent	Imperial County
Founded	1989
Headquarters	792 East Ross Road
Locale	El Centro, CA
Service type	bus service, express bus service, paratransit
Routes	9
Operator	First Transit
Web site	ivtransit.com [1]

Imperial Valley Transit is the provider of mass transportation in California's Imperial Valley, including the cities of El Centro, Calexico, and Brawley. Formed in 1989 with just 3 buses and serving just 3000 people per month, the agency currently serves more than 45,000 riders per month. Five intercity routes, plus the El Centro Circulator (which is labeled as the as Green Line running clockwise and the Blue Line running counterclockwise) travel six days per week. One limited stop route (the 600/650 Direct) also travels during weekdays, and two express buses run to Imperial Valley College when class is in session.

Routes

- 50/200: El Centro-Niland
- 100/150: El Centro-Calexico
- 300/350: El Centro-Holtville
- 400/450: El Centro-Seeley
- 500/550: Brawley-Bombay Beach
- 600/650: Brawley-Calexico Direct
- IVC Express to Niland
- IVC Express to Calexico
- Blue/Green Lines

Article Sources and Contributors

Imperial County, California *Source*: http://en.wikipedia.org/?oldid=388078280 *Contributors*: JaGa

California *Source*: http://en.wikipedia.org/?oldid=390081410 *Contributors*: Alanraywiki

Imperial Valley (California) *Source*: http://en.wikipedia.org/?oldid=384039703 *Contributors*: Insommia

Colorado Desert *Source*: http://en.wikipedia.org/?oldid=388278999 *Contributors*: Vsmith

Colorado River *Source*: http://en.wikipedia.org/?oldid=390676848 *Contributors*:

Chocolate Mountains *Source*: http://en.wikipedia.org/?oldid=389984241 *Contributors*: 1 anonymous edits

El Centro, California *Source*: http://en.wikipedia.org/?oldid=387406339 *Contributors*: 1 anonymous edits

Calexico, California *Source*: http://en.wikipedia.org/?oldid=389573087 *Contributors*: Jcmenal

Brawley, California *Source*: http://en.wikipedia.org/?oldid=377606648 *Contributors*: Michaelsbll

Imperial, California *Source*: http://en.wikipedia.org/?oldid=388970115 *Contributors*: 1 anonymous edits

Calipatria, California *Source*: http://en.wikipedia.org/?oldid=390561833 *Contributors*: R'n'B

Holtville, California *Source*: http://en.wikipedia.org/?oldid=381252882 *Contributors*: Rpyle731

Algodones Dunes *Source*: http://en.wikipedia.org/?oldid=369328292 *Contributors*: Look2See1

Salvation Mountain *Source*: http://en.wikipedia.org/?oldid=388008187 *Contributors*:

Anza-Borrego Desert State Park *Source*: http://en.wikipedia.org/?oldid=386843438 *Contributors*: Hmains

Imperial National Wildlife Refuge *Source*: http://en.wikipedia.org/?oldid=371945648 *Contributors*: Look2See1

Sonny Bono Salton Sea National Wildlife Refuge *Source*: http://en.wikipedia.org/?oldid=369240616 *Contributors*: Look2See1

Cibola National Wildlife Refuge *Source*: http://en.wikipedia.org/?oldid=384391584 *Contributors*: Look2See1

Yuma Crossing *Source*: http://en.wikipedia.org/?oldid=389832485 *Contributors*: Dondegroovily

Imperial County Airport *Source*: http://en.wikipedia.org/?oldid=382973037 *Contributors*: Aldis90

Calexico International Airport *Source*: http://en.wikipedia.org/?oldid=382973075 *Contributors*: Aldis90

Imperial Valley Transit *Source*: http://en.wikipedia.org/?oldid=380099752 *Contributors*: Look2See1

Image Sources, Licenses and Contributors

File:Map of California highlighting Imperial County.svg *Source*:
http://bibliocm.bibliolabs.com/mwAnon/index.php?title=File:Map_of_California_highlighting_Imperial_County.svg *License*: Public Domain *Contributors*:
User:Dbenbenn

File:Map of USA CA.svg *Source*: http://bibliocm.bibliolabs.com/mwAnon/index.php?title=File:Map_of_USA_CA.svg *License*: Creative Commons Attribution 2.0
Contributors: User:Huebi

File:Juan Bautista de Anza.jpg *Source*: http://bibliocm.bibliolabs.com/mwAnon/index.php?title=File:Juan_Bautista_de_Anza.jpg *License*: Public Domain *Contributors*:
Binksternet, Evrik, Scalif, Wutsje

Image:Blueangelsformationpd.jpg *Source*: http://bibliocm.bibliolabs.com/mwAnon/index.php?title=File:Blueangelsformationpd.jpg *License*: Public Domain
Contributors: Aphasic, Darz Mol, Denniss

Image:Imperial sand dunes.jpg *Source*: http://bibliocm.bibliolabs.com/mwAnon/index.php?title=File:Imperial_sand_dunes.jpg *License*: unknown *Contributors*:
Original uploader was Pretzelpaws at en.wikipedia

File:Bighorns.jpg *Source*: http://bibliocm.bibliolabs.com/mwAnon/index.php?title=File:Bighorns.jpg *License*: Creative Commons Attribution-Sharealike 2.5
Contributors: Greg Bulla. Original uploader was Gb1 at en.wikipedia

Image:I-8 (CA).svg *Source*: http://bibliocm.bibliolabs.com/mwAnon/index.php?title=File:I-8_(CA).svg *License*: Public Domain *Contributors*: User:O

Image:California 7.svg *Source*: http://bibliocm.bibliolabs.com/mwAnon/index.php?title=File:California_7.svg *License*: Public Domain *Contributors*: Geopgeop, SPUI,
Sevela.p

Image:California 78.svg *Source*: http://bibliocm.bibliolabs.com/mwAnon/index.php?title=File:California_78.svg *License*: Public Domain *Contributors*: Geopgeop,
SPUI, Sevela.p

Image:California 86.svg *Source*: http://bibliocm.bibliolabs.com/mwAnon/index.php?title=File:California_86.svg *License*: Public Domain *Contributors*: Geopgeop,
SPUI, Sevela.p

Image:California 98.svg *Source*: http://bibliocm.bibliolabs.com/mwAnon/index.php?title=File:California_98.svg *License*: Public Domain *Contributors*: Geopgeop,
SPUI, Sevela.p

Image:California 111.svg *Source*: http://bibliocm.bibliolabs.com/mwAnon/index.php?title=File:California_111.svg *License*: Public Domain *Contributors*: SPUI, The Rat
Hole 3

Image:California 115.svg *Source*: http://bibliocm.bibliolabs.com/mwAnon/index.php?title=File:California_115.svg *License*: Public Domain *Contributors*: Common
Good, SPUI

File:Flag of California.svg *Source*: http://bibliocm.bibliolabs.com/mwAnon/index.php?title=File:Flag_of_California.svg *License*: Public Domain *Contributors*:
w:en:User:DevinCookDevin Cook

File:Seal of California.svg *Source*: http://bibliocm.bibliolabs.com/mwAnon/index.php?title=File:Seal_of_California.svg *License*: Public Domain *Contributors*: Original
uploader was w:en:User:Zscout370Zscout370 at en.wikipedia

Image:Flag of California.svg *Source*: http://bibliocm.bibliolabs.com/mwAnon/index.php?title=File:Flag_of_California.svg *License*: Public Domain *Contributors*:
w:en:User:DevinCookDevin Cook

Image:Seal of California.svg *Source*: http://bibliocm.bibliolabs.com/mwAnon/index.php?title=File:Seal_of_California.svg *License*: Public Domain *Contributors*:
Original uploader was w:en:User:Zscout370Zscout370 at en.wikipedia

image:California 2.svg *Source*: http://bibliocm.bibliolabs.com/mwAnon/index.php?title=File:California_2.svg *License*: Public Domain *Contributors*: Geopgeop,
Rocket000, SPUI

image:California quarter, reverse side, 2005.jpg *Source*: http://bibliocm.bibliolabs.com/mwAnon/index.php?title=File:California_quarter,_reverse_side,_2005.jpg
License: Public Domain *Contributors*: Dbenbenn, H-stt, Huebi, Mehmet Karatay, 2 anonymous edits

File:California Map.PNG *Source*: http://bibliocm.bibliolabs.com/mwAnon/index.php?title=File:California_Map.PNG *License*: Public Domain *Contributors*: Majorly,
Severino666, Siebrand, 1 anonymous edits

Image:California Topography-MEDIUM.png *Source*: http://bibliocm.bibliolabs.com/mwAnon/index.php?title=File:California_Topography-MEDIUM.png *License*:
unknown *Contributors*: User:Ssalonen

Image:Big Sur Coast California.JPG *Source*: http://bibliocm.bibliolabs.com/mwAnon/index.php?title=File:Big_Sur_Coast_California.JPG *License*: Creative Commons
Attribution-Sharealike 3.0 *Contributors*: User:Flyer84

Image:CalaverasBigTrees2.jpg *Source*: http://bibliocm.bibliolabs.com/mwAnon/index.php?title=File:CalaverasBigTrees2.jpg *License*: Public Domain *Contributors*:
Original uploader was NX1Z at en.wikipedia

File:Mount Whitney 2003-03-25.jpg *Source*: http://bibliocm.bibliolabs.com/mwAnon/index.php?title=File:Mount_Whitney_2003-03-25.jpg *License*: Creative Commons
Attribution *Contributors*: Dbenbenn, Hike395, Zeimusu

Image:California Poppy closeup.jpg *Source*: http://bibliocm.bibliolabs.com/mwAnon/index.php?title=File:California_Poppy_closeup.jpg *License*: unknown
Contributors: Original uploader was Minesweeper at en.wikipedia

Image:Firstbearflag.jpg *Source*: http://bibliocm.bibliolabs.com/mwAnon/index.php?title=File:Firstbearflag.jpg *License*: Public Domain *Contributors*: Conscious, Epolk,
Himasaram, Homo lupus, Starscream, Valentinian, 2 anonymous edits

Image:SanFranciscoharbor1851c sharp.jpg *Source*: http://bibliocm.bibliolabs.com/mwAnon/index.php?title=File:SanFranciscoharbor1851c_sharp.jpg *License*: Public
Domain *Contributors*: Andrei Stroe, Durova, Fanque, Howcheng, Infrogmation, Kozuch, Minisarm, Romary, Scewing, 2 anonymous edits

File:Hollywood&Highland-1907.jpg *Source*: http://bibliocm.bibliolabs.com/mwAnon/index.php?title=File:Hollywood&Highland-1907.jpg *License*: Public Domain
Contributors: Fietsbel, Infrogmation, LongLiveRock, Nyttend, Werewombat

Image:California population map.png *Source*: http://bibliocm.bibliolabs.com/mwAnon/index.php?title=File:California_population_map.png *License*: GNU Free
Documentation License *Contributors*: User JimIrwin on en.wikipedia

Image:San Jose Basilica.jpg *Source*: http://bibliocm.bibliolabs.com/mwAnon/index.php?title=File:San_Jose_Basilica.jpg *License*: GNU Free Documentation License
Contributors: User:Gentgeen

CPSIA information can be obtained
at www.ICGtesting.com
Printed in the USA
LVOW05s0004010416

481629LV00022B/150/P

9 781249 221920